# DENNIS
# DOMINATOR

X20 Crewe

XBF 700S

# DENNIS
## DOMINATOR

Including associated models the Domino, Falcon and Arrow

Stewart J. Brown

Ian Allan PUBLISHING

First published 2013

ISBN 978 0 7110 3488 4

Published by Ian Allan Publishing

Printed in Malta

Distributed in the United States of America and Canada by BookMasters Distribution Services

Visit the Ian Allan Publishing website at www.ianallanpublishing.com

**FRONT COVER:** Early Dominator deliveries for Leicester City Transport included two with 77-seat Marshall bodies, the Cambridge-based builder's first double-deckers. They entered service in the summer of 1978. Stewart J. Brown

**BACK COVER:** Ayrshire independent AA Motor Services took an East Lancs-bodied Dominator in 1980. The owner was Dodds of Troon, which had previously bought Fleetlines. A second followed in 1982 and is seen outside Saltcoats station, with an earlier A1 Dominator behind. Note the differing styles of Dennis badge. Stewart J. Brown

**PAGE 1:** See page 31

**PAGE 2:** At first glance the prominent radiator grille makes this Alexander-bodied bus look like an Ailsa, but it is in fact the National Bus Company's original 1978 trial Dennis Dominator, in operation with PMT. There were some in NBC's management who objected to badges on the fronts of buses, hence the anonymous appearance of the Dominator. Cliff Beeton

**PAGE 3:** British Bus bought both Dominators and Falcons, as illustrated by this view of one of each newly delivered to North Western, at the company's Aintree depot in 1990. They had East Lancs bodies. Stewart J. Brown

**THIS PAGE:** The sign advises 'MAX. SPEED LIMIT 2 M.P.H' as a 1981 Hyndburn Dominator pauses at the exit of what was once Accrington Corporation's tram depot. Stewart J. Brown

# Contents

# Introduction

I n the mid-1970s Dennis was a small-scale builder of fire appliances and refuse-collection vehicles. It also sold trucks, but in very small numbers. In an age of gradual consolidation in the automotive industry it looked like a company with no future. It was a small business as a time when most of Britain's motor industry was part of that great product of consolidation, the British Leyland Motor Corporation. BLMC had taken over most of the big names in British car manufacturing – Austin, Daimler, Jaguar, MG, Morris, Riley, Rover, Triumph and Wolseley. And it had also acquired the big names in bus and truck building, to the point that it controlled AEC, Albion, Daimler, Guy, Scammell and, of course, Leyland. It also owned bus bodybuilders Park Royal and Roe and, in association with the National Bus Company, had an interest in Bristol and Eastern Coach Works.

BLMC's dominance of the British bus market was a cause of some concern for operators, who feared that a monopoly would restrict choice and might also see prices of vehicles and parts rise. Their fear of restricted choice was understandable in the light of Leyland's policy of encouraging operators to buy the integral Leyland National by withdrawing competing chassis models from its range.

It was this monopoly that encouraged a number of manufacturers, including Dennis, to take a fresh look at the bus business.

Some observers have described the Dennis Dominator as an updated Fleetline, which isn't necessarily an insult. The Fleetline enjoyed widespread popularity, and the Dominator used the same engine, but with a more robust gearbox which had the added benefit of an integral retarder. A number of Fleetline buyers would switch to

**ABOVE:** South Yorkshire was easily the biggest Dominator user, and most of the 322 that it operated had Alexander R-type bodies. The red and yellow Mainline livery was possibly the most attractive of the various colours they wore over the years, even in its final simplified version as seen on this 1982 bus in First ownership in Sheffield in 1999.
Tony Wilson

Dominators, including Chester, Cleveland Transit, Thamesdown and Western SMT.

The Dominator re-established Dennis as a bus builder after 10 years out of the market and paved the way for other models, including the closely associated Condor, Dragon and Falcon. And it encouraged the company to develop coach chassis, starting with the Dorchester and Lancet, which were followed by the successful and long-lived Javelin. Then came the most successful model in the company's history, the Dart.

The Dominator was pivotal in Dennis's success, and this volume looks not just at the Dominator but also at the associated models, and at the short-lived Arrow, which bridged the gap between the end of Dominator production and the introduction of another phenomenal success, the low-floor Trident.

A number of people kindly supplied information which helped in the preparation of this book. So my thanks to Andrew Braddock, David Burch, Leon Daniels, Roger Heard (who was Sales Director at Dennis for most of the period covered by this volume and with whom I had the pleasure of working in the late 1980s and 1990s), John Horn, Mark Jamieson, Barry Moore, Roger Paice and David Toy. Thanks too to the photographers who have kindly supported me; their work is credited individually.

Stewart J. Brown
Hebden Bridge
September 2012

**BELOW:** Only two operators – London & Country and Capital Citybus – bought new Dominators and new Arrows. This Dominator was one of a batch of 24 Northern Counties-bodied buses new to Capital Citybus predecessor Ensignbus. The Arrow in the background has an East Lancs body. The Dominator's livery is in accordance with Transport for London's 1997 stipulation that buses employed on contracts within its area be painted 80% red. Despite their different liveries the Dominator and the Arrow are working the same route.
Stewart J. Brown

# Chapter One
# THE BACKGROUND

Dennis had a long history in the bus business, but not always a smooth one, when it introduced its new Dominator double-decker in 1977. The company could trace its roots back to the manufacture of bicycles in Guildford in 1895, and it had been among the pioneers in the production of automobiles, producing its first motorised vehicle in 1898. It built cars, lorries and, from 1904, charabancs and, later, buses. Its first double-deckers were produced in 1911, and Dennis soon became a supplier of buses to London operators.

**ABOVE:** Between 1930 and 1954 Dennis produced small numbers of Lance double-deck chassis. The final model had a Birmingham-style 'new look' front, as seen on this 1954 East Lancs-bodied Aldershot & District bus in Reading in 1965, the last year of Lance operation by the company.
Harry Hay

What might be counted the company's first modern double-decker, the Lance, was introduced in 1930. The Lance achieved moderate success in the 1930s, notable users including Walsall Corporation and Dennis's local operator, Aldershot & District. Just over 250 Lances had been built by 1940 when war brought bus production at Dennis to an end. The Lance reappeared in 1947 and was offered with a choice of Dennis or Gardner engines. A single-deck version, the Lancet, was produced in tandem with the double-decker both before and after the war. Production of the postwar Lance came to an end in 1954, exactly 100 having been delivered to just seven operators. Easily the biggest user was Aldershot & District, with 72.

In 1955 Dennis concluded an agreement with Bristol to build the state-owned manufacturer's low-height Lodekka under licence, and this was marketed as the Loline. This did rather better than the Lance, achieving 279 sales to 15 operators, plus one demonstrator, to give a grand total of 280. In 1962 Dennis announced that it would cease Loline production – but then had a rethink and, after a gap of some 18 months, in 1964 started building the model again before finally ending production in 1967.

At this time there were five other manufacturers building double-deck bus chassis – AEC, Bristol, Daimler, Guy and Leyland. AEC and Leyland were under common ownership, and Leyland also had a minority stake in Bristol. Daimler and Guy were sister companies under Jaguar control. Consolidation of the British motor industry finally brought all of these manufacturers together, either as subsidiaries of the British Leyland Motor Corporation or, in the case of Bristol, as a part-owned business with a 50% BLMC interest.

AEC and Guy ceased building double-deck chassis at the end of the 1960s. At the start of the 1970s BLMC was involved in the three remaining double-deck chassis available in Britain. It had outright ownership of the Daimler Fleetline and Leyland Atlantean, which were built in Coventry and Leyland respectively, and its 50% interest in the Bristol VRT. The other 50% of Bristol was owned by the National Bus Company. For single-deck operation it was starting production of the Leyland National, a joint venture with NBC, hence the model's name. This was developed to replace the single-deck bus chassis produced by the various BLMC businesses – the Bristol RE, AEC Swift, Leyland Panther and Daimler Roadliner. An integral-construction vehicle with a limited range of options, it met with some resistance from operators used to buying bespoke bodywork from builders such as East Lancs and Northern Counties.

Despite the lukewarm reception afforded the National, Leyland wanted to adopt a similar policy

for double-deck buses, with a standardised integral model which it was developing as project B15, and would later launch as the Titan. That it had to rationalise and modernise its range was reasonable enough, but to offer just one model, with no choice of bodywork and a limited range of options, was not quite the way to go about it.

Which is where Dennis, since 1972 part of the Hestair group, saw an opportunity. It was not alone in seeking to challenge Leyland's market dominance. MCW had teamed up with Scania to produce the Metropolitan, unveiled in 1973. Ailsa Trucks, the Volvo truck importer, worked initially with Alexander (and later with other bodybuilders) to produce the front-engined Ailsa, also from 1973. Northern Counties established a link with truck builder Foden in 1976 to develop the Foden-NC.

Thus when the first Dominator made its appearance in 1977 it was just one of a number of attempts to provide operators with an alternative to BLMC products. An alternative was also needed by double-deck bodybuilders reliant on chassis from Daimler, Leyland and Bristol – bodybuilders whose very existence was threatened by Leyland's desire to switch from building chassis to building complete buses. And an alternative was required by many of Leyland's customers, who were being let down by late deliveries, particularly of Atlanteans and Fleetlines. These delayed deliveries were caused in part by widespread industrial unrest which led the Government to impose a three-day working week in the winter of 1973/4, to conserve energy supplies. The situation at BLMC's bus business was made worse by huge London orders for Fleetlines, as well a disruption to output when Fleetline production was moved from Coventry to Leyland in 1973.

Late deliveries were not entirely the fault of Leyland, but it was perceived as a near-monopoly supplier unable to deliver vehicles on time, and consequently it was Leyland that bore the brunt of operators' complaints. Conditions could not have been better for a new product.

ABOVE: Prior to the Dominator, Dennis's most recent double-deck model had been the Loline. Production totalled 280 over a period of nine years, and the biggest buyer was Dennis's local BET subsidiary, Aldershot & District, which took 151. This Alexander-bodied Loline III was new in 1962 and is seen in Guildford in 1973, still in traditional A&D colours but with Alder Valley fleetname in corporate NBC style.
Stewart J. Brown

ABOVE: Dennis needed publicity photographs for its first Dominator brochure, in advance of the availability of a completed bus. The answer, in the days before Photoshop made image-manipulation a simple matter, was to fit a Dennis front panel – as used on the company's goods vehicles and fire appliances – to an East Lancs-bodied bus. This 1976 Leyland Atlantean from the Brighton Corporation fleet briefly masqueraded as a Dominator. Brighton would later buy Dominators, both new and second-hand.
Stewart J. Brown collection

## Chapter Two

# THE DOMINATOR ARRIVES

Before building any chassis Dennis adopted a novel approach to testing the driveline it planned to use in its new double-deck model, the unproven combination of a Gardner 6LXB engine and a Voith automatic gearbox. In 1976 it purchased from West Yorkshire PTE a 15-year-old Daimler CVG6LX/30, into which it fitted the new drivetrain. The bus, which had been new to Leeds City Transport, had a rear-entrance Roe body. It was tried in service in 1976/7 by a few operators, including Leicester City Transport, South Yorkshire PTE and London Transport. For the last-named it was repainted from its original orange livery into overall London red.

**ABOVE:** This former Leeds City Transport Roe-bodied Daimler CVG6LX/30, new in 1959, was the unlikely starting-point for the Dominator. It was purchased by Dennis and fitted with a Gardner 6LXB engine and Voith gearbox to try out that combination in regular service. Dennis convinced London Transport to evaluate it, and in the summer of 1977 it operated alongside Routemasters on the long cross-London service between Camden Town and Richmond. Stewart J. Brown

The Gardner engine was the obvious choice for the new Dennis model. Reliable, economical and popular with fleet engineers, it powered the vast majority of Fleetlines and most Bristol VRTs. The three-speed Voith D851.2 gearbox, although little known in British buses at that time, incorporated an integral retarder, a feature which would become commonplace on 1980s urban buses. A Rolls-Royce engine was offered as an option from the start on the Dominator. Also briefly promoted in the early days was the DAF DK1160, a design developed from the Leyland 680. This was done partly with an eye on Singapore, which was running 680-engined Leyland Atlanteans. Later there would be a choice of gearboxes, in the form of a four-speed Voith D854.2, and the ZF 4HP500 four-speed and 5HP500 five-speed. There would also, briefly, be the option of a Maxwell automatic.

The standard Dominator specification included a Dennis drop-centre rear axle, allowing low-height bodywork to be fitted, and conventional leaf-spring suspension. Air suspension was quickly made available as an option and became standard in 1981, although a few operators continued to take leaf-sprung chassis – most notably Central SMT. The last chassis with leaf springs were built in 1984, for Thamesdown Transport.

There were two wheelbases. Most Dominators had the shorter, 4,953mm (16ft 3in) wheelbase, designed for an overall bodied length of around 9.5m; the long-wheelbase model, at 5,639mm (18ft 6in), was designed for 10.2m bodywork and was chosen by just a few operators. The front and rear overhangs were the same for both models, as was the gross vehicle weight, at 16.8 tonnes. There was also for a short time a choice of frame heights. The lower-built frame had a height of 527mm from the ground, compared with the standard 684mm. The frame was also slightly shallower, at 238mm against the standard 254mm. Dennis listed a left-hand-drive option for the Dominator, but none were built.

Both the West Yorkshire and South Yorkshire PTEs expressed an interest in the concept, although West Yorkshire's interest evaporated when the PTE's Engineering Director, Geoffrey Hilditch, moved to become General Manager of Leicester City Transport. Hilditch, however, maintained his support for the project, and Dennis would become the main supplier of buses to Leicester in the 1980s.

The first Dominator chassis was bodied by East Lancs, which, well aware of the threat Leyland's plans posed to its business, was looking for an alternative chassis supplier. The chassis dimensions were close to those of the Fleetline and Atlantean, and the 77-seat body fitted to the Dominator was generally similar to bodies which East Lancs was building on Atlanteans, albeit with a flush rear end,

with an inset window above the engine, and a front grille to provide ventilation for the front-mounted radiator which was a feature of the Dominator. It was bought by South Yorkshire PTE and made one of its first public appearances in the demonstration park at the Scottish Motor Show in November 1977; it then ran briefly for South Yorkshire before spending 12 months as a Dennis demonstrator. The logic behind demonstrating a bus owned by an operator was straightforward: at this time the Government was subsidising the purchase of new buses with a 50% grant towards their cost; as a manufacturer Dennis was unable to claim this, but as an operator South Yorkshire PTE could.

One other Dominator entered service in 1977, the first of an order for five with East Lancs bodies for Leicester City Transport. This order was increased before deliveries had started, and by the end of 1978 Leicester would have 26 Dominators, including two which were bodied by Marshall – the first double-deckers to be built by the Cambridge-based company. Thus in 1978 Leicester, which had previously been

**ABOVE: The first Dennis Dominator shows 001 as its route number while posed in November 1977 alongside Yorkhill Quay in Glasgow, a short distance from Kelvin Hall, where the Scottish Motor Show was being held. This South Yorkshire PTE bus was used as a Dennis demonstrator until November 1978.** Stewart J. Brown

buying Scania/MCW Metropolitans, was easily the biggest Dominator operator.

One other municipal operator took Dominators in 1978. That summer two, along with three Leyland Atlanteans, joined the East Staffordshire fleet, all five buses having East Lancs bodywork. East Staffordshire bought no more Atlanteans, but follow-on orders each year until 1981 would take its Dominator fleet to 15. When the East Staffordshire operation was taken over by Stevensons of Uttoxeter in 1985 the relatively young Dominators were quickly sold, nine going to NBC subsidiary Maidstone & District and six to Thamesdown Transport – both of which already had Dominators in their fleets.

In the 1970s the National Bus Company evaluated various new types of double-decker, and these included one Dominator. It required low-height bodywork for the bus, which was to join the PMT fleet, and this was supplied by Alexander. It was delivered to PMT at the same time as a Foden-NC. NBC ordered no more Fodens but would subsequently take another small batch of Dominators for further evaluation.

The Alexander body on the PMT Dominator was a development of the AD type fitted to Fleetlines, and a similar bus was delivered to Scottish Bus Group subsidiary Central SMT in the autumn of 1978. Central had had an unfortunate relationship with rear-engined double-deckers, first with Bristol VRTs, operated between 1969 and 1973, and then with Daimler Fleetlines, which it ran from 1971 to 1975. The Dominator followed front-engined Ailsas in the

Central fleet, and was SBG's first new Dennis. It was also the first-ever new Dennis double-decker for a Scottish operator.

The first Dominator for a Welsh operator was delivered to Cardiff City Transport in 1978, and had an East Lancs body. Destined to remain unique in the Cardiff fleet, it would be sold in 1986. It also turned out to be the only new double-deck Dominator for Wales.

From the outset Dennis promoted the Dominator as a single-decker, giving operators the chance to buy a Gardner-powered rear-engined single-decker as well as offering the benefits of standardising on the same chassis for both double- and single-deck operation. The single-deck chassis had a longer rear overhang, and the first entered service with

**ABOVE: When its demonstration period was over the original Dominator entered service with South Yorkshire, still in its cream and blue demonstration livery, as seen here in Doncaster in 1979. It received fleet livery the following year. It was to have a short life with the PTE, being sold in 1986.** Mark Bailey

**BELOW: The Dominator chassis.** Stewart J. Brown collection

Darlington Borough Transport in 1979. They had stylish 46-seat dual-door Marshall Camair 80 bodies. There were 10, a further eight following in 1980.

Hartlepool, which had standardised on Bristol REs from 1968 to 1975 and had then taken one batch of Leyland Nationals, also took single-deck Dominators in 1979. There were six, with 43-seat dual-door East Lancs bodies. These were followed by a delivery of National 2s in 1980, after which Hartlepool would return to Dennis, taking batches of Falcons.

The only new Dennises operated by Barrow Borough Transport were two single-deck Dominators with 46-seat East Lancs bodies, delivered in 1979. They joined a predominantly Leyland fleet and represented a psychological victory for Dennis in that it was supplying buses to an operator of Leyland Nationals, located just 60 miles from the National factory in Workington. They operated in Barrow until 1987/8.

The biggest Welsh buyer of the Dominator was Merthyr Tydfil Borough Transport. In 1979 the Merthyr Tydfil fleet was made up entirely of single-deckers, with a predominance of Leyland Leopards and small numbers of Bristol REs and Leyland Nationals. Six Dominators with single-deck Marshall 50-seat bodies joined the fleet in that year. They were, however, to be short-lived and were sold in 1984/5 – a six-year life, at a time when Merthyr Tydfil typically operated its vehicles for 12 years.

Lancashire municipalities generally supported Leyland, but Dennis managed to secure a handful of double-deck sales in 1979. Blackburn and Hyndburn, both of which operated East Lancs-bodied Atlanteans, took Dominators with East Lancs bodies – two for Blackburn, one for Hyndburn. It is fair to surmise that the Blackburn-based bodybuilder put pressure on its two local customers to buy the Dennises, as insurance against Leyland's plan to concentrate on selling integrals.

There were two more Scottish customers in 1979, Tayside Regional Council taking one East Lancs-bodied bus, while two were delivered to A1 Service, a co operative whose members had in the 1970s generally favoured Daimler Fleetlines. Tayside would

**LEFT:** Although built with a Gardner 6LXB engine, this 1978 Dominator for South Yorkshire PTE was quickly modified by Dennis to accept a Rolls-Royce unit, which would become the PTE standard. It was one of only three dual-door Dominators in the South Yorkshire fleet. Peter Rowlands

**BELOW:** Early Dominator deliveries for Leicester City Transport included two with 77-seat Marshall bodies, the Cambridge-based builder's first double-deckers. They entered service in the summer of 1978. Stewart J. Brown

THIS PAGE: In the summer of 1978 NBC's PMT subsidiary took delivery of a solitary Alexander-bodied Dominator, which was tested alongside a Foden-NC and a Leyland-engined Bristol VRT (above). The side advertising panel promotes the operational test. The bus later joined the Maidstone & District fleet (right). Tony Wilson (both)

take another five in 1981, while another two joined A1 in 1980 and 1981.

The first export Dominator was exhibited at the 1978 Commercial Motor Show before being delivered to China Motor Bus in Hong Kong in 1979. It had an East Lancs body into which were crammed 106 seats – quite an achievement for a two-axle double-decker. Dennis was developing new business in Hong Kong, a market which in the 1980s would become of key importance to the company. As the Dominator arrived, CMB placed an order with Dennis for 30 double-deckers – but these were front-engined Jubilants, not rear-engined Dominators. The Jubilant had been designed for operation in Hong Kong, and Dennis had supplied a trial batch of four to the Kowloon Motor Bus Co in 1977/8, which produced orders from KMB for 360 between 1979 and 1981.

Dominator deliveries were growing year on year – two in 1977, 30 in 1978, 45 in 1979 and 64 in 1980, taking the total number in service to 100 by the middle of that year. The big buyer in 1980 was Leicester, with 23, part of an ongoing intake of Dominators which in the decade that followed saw deliveries average around a dozen a year each year apart from 1987, when none was delivered.

In 1980 two other PTEs followed South Yorkshire's lead in purchasing small numbers of Dominators for evaluation. Merseyside took five with 78-seat Willowbrook bodies, while two were delivered to Greater Manchester; these were the first to be bodied by Northern Counties, the main body supplier to Greater Manchester, with its Wigan factory in the PTE's operating area. Merseyside took 10 more Dominators, but with Alexander bodies, in 1982. Greater Manchester added a further pair of Northern Counties-bodied buses in 1981. The four Greater Manchester Dominators would be withdrawn in 1986 as part of a massive cull of old and non-standard vehicles, prompted by the deregulation of local bus services; they were sold to Whippet of Fenstanton.

There were three new municipal customers in 1980. Most new buses delivered to Derby in the 1970s had been Fleetlines, but towards the end of the decade the operator did try other types – a low-height Ailsa in 1977, a Foden-NC in 1978 and an MCW Metrobus in 1980. Also delivered to Derby in 1980 were three Dominators with Marshall bodies, similar to those in service in Leicester. They were followed in 1981 by three more, this time bodied by Northern Counties. All six would be withdrawn in 1986, as Derby rationalised its fleet in the face of deregulation. The three Northern Counties-bodied buses were sold to Thamesdown, while the three with Marshall bodies went to Citybus in Hong Kong.

ABOVE: The first new Dennis double-decker for a Scottish operator was delivered to Central SMT towards the end of 1978. The 74-seat Alexander body was of an interim style used only on two Dominators (the other being the PMT bus illustrated opposite) pending the introduction of the new R-type in 1979. This is a mid-1980s view in Glasgow. When new the bus was painted all-over red with just a single band of cream relief above the lower-deck windows. It originally had a grille similar to that of the PMT bus, but by the time of this photograph it had acquired an Ailsa grille.
Stewart J. Brown

Cleveland Transit, another Fleetline buyer, took two Northern Counties-bodied Dominators in 1980. It would still be placing Fleetlines in service as late as 1983 – the last operator to do so – at which time it turned to Dennis, taking a dozen Dominators in 1983/4, followed by five in 1985 and four in 1986. All had Northern Counties bodywork.

The third new municipal buyer in 1980 was Thamesdown Transport. Thamesdown wanted more Bristol REs, to add to the five it was already running, but Leyland could only offer Nationals. So Thamesdown instead purchased four single-deck Dominators with 40-seat Marshall bodies, of a similar design to those in service with Darlington and Merthyr Tydfil but shorter, as they had the same rear overhang as on double-deck chassis rather than the longer overhang normally used for single-deckers. They were the last single-deck Dominators, bringing the total to just 36. The introduction of a new purpose-designed rear-engined single-deck chassis, the Falcon with a

horizontal Gardner 6HLXB engine, had rendered the Dominator single-decker redundant.

The purchase of new double-deckers by independent operators was slowing down at the start of the 1980s as the Government was phasing out its capital grant for new bus purchases. Nevertheless, one old-established English independent, OK Motor Services of Bishop Auckland, took a long-wheelbase Dominator with 85-seat Northern Counties body in 1980. In Scotland AA Motor Services followed A1's lead, taking delivery of an East Lancs-bodied Dominator in 1980; it added another in 1982.

The associated Doncaster independent operators Blue Line and Reliance each ordered one Dominator. Both ran Fleetlines. However, the two businesses were bought by South Yorkshire PTE in 1979, and the Dominators were delivered to the PTE in 1980, with PTE-style dual-door East Lancs bodies. One had a Maxwell gearbox, which would be replaced by a standard Voith unit later in the vehicle's life. The Maxwell gearbox was briefly offered as an option on the Dominator.

**ABOVE: Darlington Borough Transport was the first operator of single-deck Dominators. It had 18, the first 10 entering service in 1979. They had 46-seat Marshall Camair 80 bodywork. This is a September 1979 view.**
Stewart J. Brown

NBC subsidiary Maidstone & District was involved in the testing of non-standard vehicle types and in 1980 received six Dominators with full-height Willowbrook bodies. These had originally been intended for Alder Valley (which as successor to Aldershot & District was no stranger to Dennis products), but this plan was revised before the buses were delivered. While no more new Dominators were bought by NBC, Maidstone & District would at the end of 1985 buy nine former East Staffordshire examples when that operation was acquired by Stevensons of Uttoxeter. The solitary PMT Dominator also joined the M&D fleet.

The only Dominator built for non-PSV operation was a long-wheelbase model bodied by Angloco in 1980 for use by the Tyne & Wear Metropolitan Fire Brigade as an incident command unit. It was to serve the brigade until 2002, in the interim covering just 35,000 miles.

In 1981 Dominator annual deliveries topped the 100 mark for the first time, a total of 127 being delivered to 13 operators. The most significant of these was South Yorkshire PTE, which took 55 with Alexander bodies – part of a 174-vehicle order which was fulfilled between May 1981 and December 1982. The first arrived as the PTE was receiving its last Atlanteans. South Yorkshire selected Rolls-Royce rather than Gardner engines and also specified single-door bodywork with 78 seats; until this time most of the PTE's double-deckers had been of dual-door layout. In place of the Dennis drop-centre rear axle the South Yorkshire buses used a GKN Kirkstall straight axle, which unit ultimately became the standard.

Central SMT, which had taken an early Dominator in 1978, placed an order for 20 in 1981. These had low-height Alexander R-type bodies, with 76 seats. Fifteen were to Dennis's standard specification, with Gardner engines and Voith D851 gearboxes, but the remaining five were the first Rolls-Royce-engined double-deckers in Scotland; four of them had Voith gearboxes, the fifth had a Maxwell gearbox. Central would become Dennis's biggest Scottish Dominator

**THIS PAGE:** The East Lancs single-deck body for the Dominator was quite an attractive vehicle from the front, as seen on this bus, one of six supplied to Hartlepool Borough Transport in 1979. But confronted with a single-deck chassis with a vertical rear engine East Lancs clearly did not know quite how to style the back end of its bodywork. The result is a bus which looks as though a powerpack has been hung onto the end of the body. Note also the long rear overhang of the single-deck **Dominator.** Mark Bailey, David Cole

**ABOVE:** Barrow Borough Transport took just two Dominators, and these had East Lancs single-deck bodies which were similar to those on the Hartlepool buses but of single- rather than dual-door layout. New in 1979, they were withdrawn in 1987/8 and sold for scrap. Tony Greaves

customer, repeat orders for Gardner-powered buses, delivered in 1982 and 1983, taking its fleet to 51.

There were another three new municipal buyers in 1981. Chester City Transport's standard bus in the 1970s had been the Fleetline, and when that model was dropped Chester switched to the Dominator – precisely the sort of customer Dennis had been seeking. Five were delivered in 1981, a further six following in 1982, and a final three in 1983; all were bodied by Northern Counties. The 1981 and 1982 deliveries replaced the last of Chester's Guy Arabs. In 1985 Chester reverted to Leyland products, taking four Olympians, but in the same year it also acquired three of Merthyr Tydfil's redundant Dominator single-deckers, which replaced high-floor Leyland Leopards; by 1980s standards the Dominators were low-floor buses. This made Chester one of the few operators to run both single- and double-deck Dominators.

In 1979/80 Brighton Borough Transport had borrowed two Dominators – a South Yorkshire Rolls-Royce-engined bus and a Gardner-powered vehicle from East Staffordshire. Comparative trials of these two buses were carried out along with a South Yorkshire Leyland Atlantean with a Voith gearbox, and one of Brighton's own AN68 Atlanteans. In terms of fuel economy the Rolls-Royce Dominator was worst, managing just 5.3mpg. Next came the Voith-equipped AN68 (5.4mpg) and the standard AN68 (6.4mpg), the East Staffordshire Dominator giving the best fuel figure, 7.6mpg. Brighton ordered two Dominators, which were delivered in 1981 with bodywork by East Lancs, at that time Brighton's preferred builder. Along the coast Eastbourne Borough Council took four Dominators in 1981 and a further five in 1982. Like Brighton, Eastbourne had previously bought Atlanteans and was an established East Lancs customer.

**ABOVE:** Leyland had a strong grip when it came to selling buses to Lancashire municipalities, and Blackburn's order for Dominators in 1979 – the first from an operator in the North West of England – must have caused not a little dismay in Leyland's boardroom. It was only for two buses and, as it transpired, it didn't lead to massive ongoing business for Dennis. They were bodied by East Lancs, a significant employer in the town. Here one tackles the East Park Road hill on its way from the town centre to Revidge in 1981. Stewart J. Brown

**RIGHT:** A solitary Dominator with East Lancs body was delivered to Tayside Regional Council in 1979. A further five followed in 1981, but Tayside's preferred choice at this time was the Ailsa. This is the original vehicle, seen in Dundee in the summer of 1981. Tayside would sell its Dennises in 1985, most passing to Brighton Borough Transport, but this one was destined to end up with Citybus in Hong Kong. Stewart J. Brown

The first Dominators for an independent operator were two East Lancs-bodied examples which entered service with A1 Service of Ardrossan in 1979. Here one heads through Saltcoats shortly after delivery.
Stewart J. Brown

BELOW; The biggest buyer of new Dominators in Wales was Merthyr Tydfil Borough Transport. Six were delivered in 1979, with stylish Marshall Camair 80 bodywork seating 50. Stewart J. Brown

ABOVE; The first Willowbrook-bodied Dominators were six 75-seaters for NBC's Maidstone & District company, delivered in 1980. One is seen leaving the Pentagon bus station in Chatham. The only other Dominators with Willowbrook bodies were five for Merseyside PTE.
Stewart J. Brown

LEFT: East Staffordshire bought 15 Dominators with East Lancs bodies between 1978 and 1981. They were the fleet's last new buses. When the operation was taken over by Stevensons of Uttoxeter in 1985 the Dominators were quickly sold to Maidstone & District and Thamesdown Transport. Peter Rowlands

**LEFT:** The first five Dominators for Merseyside PTE were purchased for evaluation in 1980. They had 78-seat Willowbrook bodies and were numbered in the 00xx series, which also included trial batches of Ailsas, MCW Metrobuses and Leyland Olympians. This is a 1981 view in Liverpool. Stewart J. Brown

**RIGHT:** OK Motor Services was the first English independent to take delivery of a Dominator, placing a long-wheelbase Northern Counties-bodied bus in service in the early months of 1980. Seating 85, the highest capacity thus far for a home-market Dominator, it was also one of very few examples to be crew-operated; the conductress is standing by the door in this photograph taken when the bus was new. Latterly painted in a simplified livery, it would be sold at the end of the decade, to Chester City Transport. Tony Greaves

**LEFT:** The first Northern Counties-bodied Dominators were two for Greater Manchester PTE, delivered in the spring of 1980. They were 75-seaters and are seen here posed in central Manchester for Dennis's photographer. Dennis

**LEFT:** Ayrshire independent AA Motor Services took an East Lancs-bodied Dominator in 1980. The owner was Dodds of Troon, which had previously bought Fleetlines. A second followed in 1982 and is seen outside Saltcoats station, with an earlier A1 Dominator behind. Note the differing styles of Dennis badge. Stewart J. Brown

**BELOW:** In 1980 Derby City Transport received three Dominators with Marshall bodies, generally similar to the two delivered to Leicester in 1978. Only 10 Dominators had double-deck Marshall bodies, all the others being at Leicester. The orange band above the windscreen indicated a one-man-operated bus. Stewart J. Brown collection

**ABOVE:** Two Dominators with East Lancs bodies joined the South Yorkshire PTE fleet in 1980. They had been ordered by Doncaster independents Samuel Morgan and R. Store, whose businesses were purchased by the PTE in 1979. This one is seen in Sheffield in 1981. David Cole

**RIGHT:** The last single-deck Dominators were four for Thamesdown Transport, delivered in the summer of 1980. They had Marshall Camair 80 bodies, similar to those supplied to Darlington and Merthyr Tydfil. This style of body was fitted to 28 of the 36 Dominators that were bodied as single-deckers. Stewart J. Brown

**ABOVE:** The only dedicated Dominator demonstrator was the original South Yorkshire vehicle which operated in Hestair Dennis livery. However, Dennis did on occasion borrow customers' vehicles, as shown in this view of a 1980 Leicester bus running for Strathclyde PTE in January 1981. It had an East Lancs body and was the first air-suspended Dominator. Stewart J. Brown

**ABOVE:** From 1981 the Dominator was in effect the South Yorkshire PTE's standard double-decker, with a Rolls-Royce engine, Voith gearbox and air suspension. The first 174, delivered in 1981/2, had 78-seat Alexander RH bodies. This example is seen in Sheffield wearing the original livery applied to the type. Stewart J. Brown

**LEFT:** From late 1985 South Yorkshire PTE added red to its livery, transforming the appearance of the fleet. It also adopted 'South Yorkshire's Transport' as its fleetname. The effect can be seen on an Alexander-bodied Dominator in Sheffield bus station. Stewart J. Brown

**LEFT:** In 1981 Central SMT took 20 Dominators with low-height Alexander R-type bodies, following the trial vehicle delivered in 1978. One is seen in East Kilbride in 1984. Central would build up a fleet of 50 Dominators with R-type bodies. Stewart J. Brown

**BELOW:** Following its purchase in 1980 of three Dominators with Marshall bodies, Derby City Transport took another three in 1981, but this time bodied by Northern Counties. In 1986 the trio joined the Thamesdown fleet; this one, still in Derby livery, is seen in central Swindon soon after acquisition. David Cole

**LEFT:** Eastbourne Borough Council bought nine East Lancs-bodied Dominators in 1981/2. Eastbourne had previously bought Atlanteans, and after the Dominators it would return to Leyland, with orders for Olympians. Peter Rowlands

**RIGHT:** Further along the South Coast, Brighton Borough Transport also bought East Lancs-bodied Dominators, taking two in 1981. The previous Brighton standard is represented here by two Atlanteans in the background. Stewart J. Brown

**LEFT:** In 1982 Merseyside PTE received a second batch of Dominators – 10 with Alexander R-type bodies. They took to 15 the number n service and were the PTE's last deliveries of the type. Pier Head was for many years one of the main terminal points for buses in Liverpool. Stewart J. Brown

## Chapter Three
# GROWING SUCCESS IN THE 1980s

By 1982 Dennis was doing quite nicely in Hong Kong. Admittedly there was just one Dominator in operation, with CMB, but there were almost 400 front-engined Jubilants. These were not the most sophisticated of buses, but they provided both CMB and the territory's other main operator, KMB, with levels of reliability which had been lacking in their rear-engined Fleetlines. During 1982 CMB added a further six Dominators with dual-door, low-height Alexander R type bodies – three with leaf springs and three with air suspension.

**ABOVE:** In the period 1981-3 Chester City Transport purchased 14 new Dominators with Northern Counties bodies, and these would later be joined by second-hand Dominators from a wide range of operators. A 1982 bus is seen when new outside Chester Cathedral. Stewart J. Brown

Both CMB and KMB were looking for maximum-capacity buses, and this saw their British chassis suppliers developing new three-axle models. The first three-axle Ailsas and MCW Metrobuses entered service in 1981, to be followed by Leyland's first three-axle Olympian in 1982. Dennis duly developed a three-axle version of the Dominator and in 1982 supplied three to KMB and two to CMB. As delivered to KMB this model was known as the Dragon – a name with obvious Oriental connotations – while those supplied to CMB were Condors. The three-axle chassis was offered in two lengths, 11m and 12m. The addition of a third axle increased the gross weight from 16.8 to just under 22 tonnes. The turbocharged 230bhp Gardner 6LXCT was the standard unit, on the basis that the 188bhp 6LXB would have insufficient power to cope with a fully loaded bus in the challenging operating conditions in Hong Kong. There were also two 250bhp options – the Cummins L10 and the Gardner 6LXDT. The L10 (though not the 6LXDT) would also be made available in the UK.

The two-axle Dominator sold in small numbers in Hong Kong, a total of seven being supplied to CMB, and one batch of 40 to KMB. But the three-axle

chassis achieved amazing success. By the end of the 1980s there would be 460 running in Hong Kong, the majority with KMB. A few early examples were dual-door 127-seaters, but most 1980s Dragons seated around 108 with either two- or three-door bodywork by Duple Metsec, a sister company of Dennis within the Hestair group.

A solitary East Lancs-bodied DAF-engined Dominator was supplied to Singapore Bus Service in 1982, but here Dennis was unable to repeat its Hong Kong success. The SBS Dominator remained a one-off.

In 1982 Thamesdown, which was already running four single-deck Dominators, became the only operator to buy new double-deck as well as new single-deck models. Thamesdown was a Fleetline operator, and the five Northern Counties-bodied Dominators delivered in 1982 established a pattern for future deliveries, similar buses being delivered each year until 1985, by which time Thamesdown was running 19. There then came a temporary halt in the purchase of new double-deckers as the operator faced the uncertainty of the impending deregulated environment. It did, however, add nine used Dominators to its fleet in 1985/6, from East Staffordshire and Derby.

**ABOVE: Just one Dominator, a long-wheelbase model, was supplied to Singapore Bus Service, in 1982. It had a 79-seat East Lancs body with deep-sliding side windows and an opening section in the driver's windscreen. It was the only Dominator to be powered by a DAF engine, the 11.6-litre DK1160, driving through the standard Voith gearbox; the small badge under the nearside headlights reads 'DAF Diesel'. The bus ran in Singapore for only 12 months before being shipped to Hong Kong, where it was used as a training bus by KMB.**
Alan Mortimer

in Britain was shrinking dramatically, being hit not only by the withdrawal of New Bus Grant but also by the threat posed by the deregulation of local bus services, which for a few years in the mid-1980s would see many operators investing in minibuses rather than double-deckers.

The supply of Rolls-Royce-powered Dominators to South Yorkshire continued apace, 30 Alexander-bodied buses being delivered in 1983, and 49 in 1984. Alongside what could be considered its standard Alexander-bodied buses the PTE took 10 with Northern Counties bodies in 1983 and 15 with East Lancs bodies in 1984. In the interests of standardisation both bodies shared features with the R-type, and the East Lancs examples were a pretty close copy, all but indistinguishable from the genuine Alexander product.

The 500th Dominator – the last of a batch of 10 for Central SMT – entered service in 1983. To sell 500 buses in seven years was no mean feat, and one significantly better than had been managed by any previous generation of Dennis double-decker. Compared with the other manufacturers which could be regarded as newcomers to the market, it was a better performance than was being achieved by Ailsa, although it lagged a long way behind MCW, whose Metrobus sales were boosted by huge orders from London Transport and West Midlands PTE.

Western SMT followed Central SMT in ordering Dominators, taking 12 in 1983, including two with Maxwell gearboxes, for operation in Greenock. Since 1965 Western had generally favoured Fleetlines. A further 12 Dominators were ordered for 1985, but by the time these were delivered the Greenock

Warrington Borough Transport ran Atlanteans, and in 1982 it took two Olympians and four Dominators. It would buy more of each, including four more Dominators in 1983, before standardising on the Dennis model later in the decade.

With 192 Dominators entering service in Britain, 1982 was easily the model's best year. More than half – 119 – were for South Yorkshire, while other big customers were Leicester and Central SMT, each taking 20. An oddity among Leicester's buses was one with a Maxwell gearbox which was an exhibit at the 1982 Motor Show.

Never again would more than 100 Dominators enter service in any one year. Demand for new buses

**ABOVE: Between 1980 and 1986 Cleveland Transit built up a fleet of 23 Dominators with low-height Northern Counties bodies. This example, loading in Stockton High Street, was one of 10 delivered during the winter of 1983/4.**
Stewart J. Brown

operations of Western were under the control of the new Clydeside Scottish company, which inherited the 12 buses delivered in 1983 and received the 1985 delivery as its first new vehicles. The Clydeside buses were the last new Dominators for a Scottish operator. A total of 87 new Dominators were supplied to Scottish companies – 75 Alexander-bodied buses for SBG, plus six with East Lancs bodies for Ayrshire independents A1 and AA, and six for Tayside, also bodied by East Lancs.

At the start of the 1980s Southampton City Transport had a highly standardised double-deck fleet made up solely of East Lancs-bodied Atlanteans. In 1984 it took one Dominator and three Leyland Olympians for evaluation. Four more Dominators (and four more Olympians) followed in 1986. Then, in 1988, Southampton took eight more Dominators – its last new double-deckers. All of these buses had East Lancs bodies.

Kingston-upon-Hull joined the ranks of Dominator buyers in 1984, taking 10 with Alexander R-type bodies. They were followed in 1985/6 by a further 15 Dominators. Twelve of these were outwardly similar to the R-types but were in fact bodied by East Lancs; the other three had East Lancs' coach-style body, with curved windscreens. These in turn were joined by more Dominators – two batches of 10 in 1987 and 1988 and a final six in 1989, all with the East Lancs version of Alexander's body. The sixteen delivered in 1988/9 had Cummins engines.

One 1984 delivery which Dennis must have been hoping would further boost its fortunes was of three Dominators to London Transport. These had dual-door

bodywork by Northern Counties and were evaluated alongside three Leyland Olympians, three Ailsas and two MCW Metrobus Mk IIs. Delivered in November 1984, they entered service from Stockwell garage in February 1985. All had the standard 170bhp Gardner 6LXB engine. Two also had the standard Voith D851 gearbox, but the third had a Maxwell unit. Having latterly been adorned with South London subsidiary fleetnames, they were in 1991 converted to single-door and transferred to the London Coaches fleet. Two were sold to Capital Citybus in 1993. Dennis would in fact soon become a major supplier of buses to London – but not with the Dominator.

A less hopeful prospect was a trolleybus. This was developed for South Yorkshire PTE, and the chassis, with a GEC traction motor mounted in the rear overhang, was exhibited at the 1984 Motor Show. A three-cylinder auxiliary Dorman 3DA air-cooled diesel engine was fitted so that the bus could move short distances under its own power. The trolleybus chassis was fitted with an 80-seat Alexander body and delivered to the PTE in August 1985. Overhead wiring was erected at Doncaster Racecourse so that the vehicle, promoted as Electroline, could be demonstrated. The project, launched when deregulation was approaching, was doomed from the outset. The last trolleybus to be built in Britain, it was retained by the PTE when it set up a separate operating company, South Yorkshire Transport, to run its buses after deregulation. The bus never operated in revenue-earning service, and has been preserved at the Sandtoft Trolleybus Museum.

There was, incidentally, one other Dennis trolleybus. In 2001 Citybus, in Hong Kong, converted a

upon-Trent Corporation in 1968. Gardner claimed that
fuel consumption for the 5LXCT would be around
7.0mpg compared with 6.3mpg for a 6LXB. Another
Gardner alternative was the turbocharged 6LXCT
rated at either 230 or 242bhp, compared with 188bhp
for the standard 6LXB. Dennis also acknowledged the
growing popularity of the Cummins L10 and offered
that too, with 180 and 215bhp power ratings.

In 1988 Dennis announced a five-year 65-bus
order for Dominators for Leicester City Bus. The first
two years' orders were delivered – 13 buses in 1988
and a further 13 in 1989, with 215bhp Cummins L10
engines and Voith gearboxes. But these turned out
to be Leicester's last new Dominators; the
outstanding 39 were never delivered, although
Leicester did receive 16 Falcons in the period 1991-3.

During the 1980s there was some interest among
municipal fleets in coach operation, and a number
took coach-seated double-deckers, which offered
varying degrees of luxury. The first of Ipswich's two
Dominators had been fitted with coach seats, and
some of the vehicles supplied to Brighton, Hull and
Thamesdown were similarly equipped. Warrington
went further and had two of the six long-wheelbase
Dominators delivered in 1988 fitted-out as 76-seaters
(compared with 88 seats in its four buses), included
Girling Skidcheck in the chassis specification, and
painted them in the company's blue CoachLines livery.

As NBC was privatised in the second half of the
1980s, so new names appeared in the bus industry.
One of these was Drawlane, which owned London
Country South West. A striking 76-seat long-
wheelbase East Lancs-bodied Dominator coach for
LCSW was exhibited at the 1988 Motor Show. Fitted
with Gardner's more powerful 6LXCT engine in place
of the standard 6LXB, it was followed in the spring of
1989 by a further eight Dominators – seven standard-
length 76-seaters (primarily for operation on London
Transport route 131 between Weybridge and Kingston)
and one long wheelbase 84-seater. The original
vehicle was refitted as a 78-seat bus in 1992, after
operating for a short time in Green Line coach livery.

For 1989 Drawlane also ordered seven Dominators
for its North Western company and three for Midland
Red North, but in the event all 10 were delivered to
North Western. The group's 1990 Dominator order
comprised eight for Crosville, four for North Western
and two for Midland Red North, but by the time these
were delivered Drawlane had reorganised its
operations, part of the Crosville business being taken
over by Midland Red North. Consequently the buses
were delivered to North Western (eight) and Midland
Red North (six). Drawlane at this time owned East
Lancs, so, unsurprisingly, all of the Dominators had
East Lancs bodies. The 1990 vehicles were
noteworthy through being built to a lower-than-
normal height of 13ft 9in.

1994 Dragon to electric propulsion. The bus had a
Duple Metsec body, assembled by Caetano, which
required strengthening of the roof to support the
trolley booms. Overhead wiring was installed at a
short test track in one of the company's depots. It was
no more successful than the South Yorkshire bus.

Dennis secured just one big Dominator order for
1985, 30 being delivered to Greater Manchester PTE.
These followed four trial vehicles supplied in 1980/1.
They were initially allocated to depots in Rochdale,
Bolton, Oldham and Manchester (Northenden) and
were bodied by Northern Counties, which had been
in PTE ownership since 1983. However, by 1985 the
Leyland Olympian was established as the PTE's
standard double-decker, with over 150 in service by
the time the Dominators arrived.

Ipswich, with a double-deck fleet made up mainly of
Atlanteans, and a new operational policy which was
focussed on single-deckers, took one Dominator (and
one Leyland Olympian) in 1985, with a Gardner 6LXB
engine and a Maxwell gearbox that would later be
replaced by Voith transmission. A second Dominator
was delivered in 1988. Both buses had dual-door East
Lancs bodies, by this time an unusual layout for a small
fleet. The first was particularly unusual in having a
single-width entrance door, a feature associated with
buses for Nottingham City Transport and Hong Kong.
Both later passed to other municipally-owned fleets,
the first, rebuilt with a standard-width entrance, seeing
further service with Eastbourne Buses, the second with
Thamesdown. Both also had their centre exits removed.

Leicester was taking batches of Dominators each
year, and two of those delivered in 1985 had Gardner
5LXCT engines, making them the first new five-
cylinder-engined buses to enter service in Britain
since a trio of Daimler CCG5s delivered to Burton-

**ABOVE AND LEFT:** Western SMT followed sister Scottish Bus Group company Central in specifying Alexander-bodied Dominators. Twelve were delivered in 1983, joining a double-deck fleet made up largely of Fleetlines. They were based in Greenock. A further 12, ordered for 1985, were delivered to the new Clydeside Scottish company, which that year had taken over Western's Greenock operations. One of the first batch is seen following repaint but before application of the Clydeside name (above). By 1991 Western was back in Greenock and the Dominators had been repainted in the company's unusual white-based livery (above right).

Stewart J. Brown, Peter Rowlands

ABOVE: Between 1978 and 1986 South Yorkshire PTE placed in service 322 Dominators – just under one-third of the total number delivered to British operators. Most had Alexander bodywork as fitted to this 1983 bus in Mainline livery, the identity adopted from 1989 for the PTE's bus company.
Stewart J. Brown

did buy new Dominators. Ensignbus took 24, with dual-door 76-seat Northern Counties bodies, in the winter of 1990/1 for operation on London Transport services in East London. These were the last dual-door Dominators for UK service; the only other British buyers of dual-door double-deck Dominators were South Yorkshire PTE (three), Tayside (six), London (three) and Ipswich (two). Ensignbus had previously bought MCW Metrobuses with Gardner engines and Voith gearboxes. With MCW having ceased bus building, the Dominator provided Ensign with the same driveline as was fitted to its Metrobuses.

The Ensignbus business was bought by the owner of Hong Kong Citybus at the end of 1990 and re-branded as Capital Citybus. Later that year a further two Dominators were delivered to Capital Citybus, in its new yellow livery. One was the first bus to be powered by the new 12.7-litre 210bhp Gardner LG1200 engine and was an exhibit at the Coach & Bus '91 show at the National Exhibition Centre. The other Capital Citybus bus had a Cummins L10, and an L10 was later used to replace the engine in the LG1200-powered bus. The LG1200 engine was also fitted to a batch of 25 Dragons for KMB.

Greater Manchester Buses, the PTE-owned company formed in 1986, took 10 Dominators with 6LXCT engines and four-speed Voith D854 gearboxes in 1991 (alongside 10 Volvo Citybuses and five Scania N113s). At this point it reallocated its 30 existing Dominators, so that all 40 Dennis double-deckers were based at its Princess Road depot in Manchester. When GM Buses was privatised they passed to the GM Buses South company.

By now Dominator sales were waning. From 46 deliveries in 1991 the figure dropped to just eight –

Dominator deliveries in the 1980s reached a low of just 10 – for Kingston-upon-Hull – in 1987. They did recover, but not by much, the post-deregulation high being 46, in 1989. In that year Dennis secured a new municipal customer, Grimsby-Cleethorpes Transport. It took an initial four, and follow-on orders brought the total to 15 by 1992. The first seven, in 1989/90, had 78-seat Alexander R-type bodies; the other eight had East Lancs copies of the R-type but with BET-style curved windscreens, and, on the last four, split-step entrances designed to improve accessibility.

The last municipal operator to convert to the Dominator was Bournemouth Transport, which in the years 1990-2 took 18, all bodied by East Lancs in the Alexander style.

While the three trial buses for London Transport had not produced any orders, one London operator

RIGHT: Kowloon Motor Bus ordered 40 Dominators, which entered service in 1984 and had 92-seat Duple Metsec bodies. Dennis's real success with KMB in the 1980s and 1990s would be in the supply of three-axle Dragons.
Stewart J. Brown

four each for Bournemouth and Grimsby-Cleethorpes – in 1992. In 1993 just three Dominators were delivered. These had been ordered by Strathclyde Buses, but that operator cancelled them, and they were purchased by Mayne of Manchester. They had East Lancs bodies.

And that was almost the end. No Dominators were built in 1994 or 1995, and the last were produced in 1996 – four for Guildford & West Surrey, part of British Bus (the name adopted by the former Drawlane business in 1992). They were ordered for a route between Guildford and Camberley with limited clearance on which the company could not operate the higher-built Arrow, 10 of which were bought at the same time for the main London & Country operation. They had Cummins L10 engines and ZF gearboxes.

The Guildford & West Surrey buses brought to 1,007 the number of Dominators built. This figure included one trolleybus, 48 export sales and a fire service control vehicle; the 957 motor buses built for operation in Britain comprised 921 double-deckers and 36 single-deckers.

Five companies supplied British bus operators with bodywork for the Dominator. With 396 (including the trolleybus) Alexander was the biggest, thanks in no small part to orders from South Yorkshire PTE (294) and the Scottish Bus Group (75). Next came East Lancs, which supplied 370 bodies (including eight single-deckers) to a much wider range of operators; it also enjoyed the distinction of having bodied both the first Dominator, in 1977, and the last, in 1996. Northern Counties bodied 143 Dominators, Marshall 38 (of which 28 were single deckers), and Willowbrook 11.

Yet to look at the Dominator without taking into account export sales of the three-axle version is to underplay the success achieved by Dennis. Between 1982 and 1999 the company produced an impressive 2,106 three-axle Dragons and Condors, primarily for Hong Kong, but with small numbers going to Stagecoach in Malawi, becoming that country's first new double-deck buses, and to Kenya, where they reintroduced double-deck operation after a break of almost 20 years. Add these to the total and the combined figure for two-axle and three-axle versions of what was in essence the same chassis becomes 3,113 – which in terms of double-deck chassis production in the 1980s and 1990s places the Dominator range second only to Leyland's Olympian.

**ABOVE: In the years 1982-5 Thamesdown Transport bought 19 new Dominators with Northern Counties bodies. Here a 1984 bus at London's Victoria Coach Station on hire to National Express offers Birmingham passengers a rather less luxurious mode of travel than they might have expected.** Tony Wilson

**LEFT: A council-wide corporate livery was adopted for Leicester City Transport's fleet in 1984, with a new Leicester City Bus name. It is seen here on a 1984 Dominator with East Lancs' later style of four-bay bodywork with curved windscreens, fitted to this and subsequent Dominator deliveries for Leicester. This is a 1986 view, and the bus displays 'No Fuss. Go CityBus.' decals reflecting competition from Midland Fox, which operator's Fox Cub minibuses can be seen snapping at its heels.** Stewart J. Brown

**ABOVE:** Kingston-upon-Hull City Transport joined the ranks of municipal Dominator customers in 1984, 10 Alexander-bodied buses entering service at the end of that year. One is seen in the summer of 1985. Most of Hull's Dominators had this style of bodywork, although subsequent deliveries were built by East Lancs rather than Alexander. David Cole

**RIGHT:** It might look like just another standard South Yorkshire Dominator bodied by Alexander, but this 1984 bus was one of 15 that were bodied by East Lancs to Alexander's R-type design. This meant that the PTE did not have to stock different sizes of glass and different body mouldings when it came to repairing a damaged bus. Peter Rowlands

**THIS PAGE:** Ten Dominators with Northern Counties bodies were purchased by South Yorkshire PTE in 1984. The bodies were built to match the operator's preferred design, the Alexander R-type, but the front dome was of typical Northern Counties style. One is seen in its original livery in Sheffield's Pond Street bus station in 1985 (above), while a 1999 view (below), also in Sheffield, shows another towards the end of its life, in Mainline livery with the addition of First fleetnames. David Cole, Tony Wilson

LEFT: Southampton City Transport's first Dominator was a one-off vehicle delivered in 1984. It had a 76-seat body by East Lancs, which by this time had been Southampton's main body supplier for the best part of 20 years. Peter Rowlands

BELOW: Three Dominators ordered by South Yorkshire were diverted to Leicester City Bus in 1984 in exchange for three Dennis Dorchester coaches. Although bodied by East Lancs, like the vast majority of Leicester's Dominators, they were the only examples in the fleet built to the Alexander R-type design. Tony Wilson

**LEFT AND ABOVE:** After taking two Dominators in 1981 Brighton bought just four more, in 1985. Like the original pair the follow-on order had East Lancs bodies – two buses (left) and two coaches (above). The coach displays a cheery message. These were the operator's last new double-deckers and would be withdrawn in 1996. Peter Rowlands, Tony Wilson

**BELOW:** As well as buying four new Dominators, in 1985 Brighton bought Tayside's five long-wheelbase buses, which dated from 1981. These had East Lancs bodies, albeit with curved windscreens, and fitted easily into the Brighton fleet. They were withdrawn in 1990/1, following which four would see further service with Chester City Transport and another with Eastbourne Buses. Peter Rowlands

**ABOVE:** It might be branded 'The quiet revolution in transport', but the trolleybus revolution never came about. South Yorkshire PTE took delivery of this Alexander-bodied Dominator-based trolleybus in 1985 and built a short demonstration loop close to its Doncaster depot, where it is seen in 1986. A quarter of a century later the bus is a museum-piece, at Sandtoft. *Stewart J. Brown*

**RIGHT:** At the start of 1986 Hull added 15 Dominators to its fleet, with East Lancs bodies. Twelve were 75-seat Alexander R-type look-alikes, virtually indistinguishable from 10 Falkirk-built buses delivered in 1984, but three were specified as 71-seat coaches and had curved windscreens on both decks. The original 'Kingstonian' coach branding has given way to 'Blue & Whites' in this early-1990s view. The coaches had Gardner 6LXCT engines; the buses the standard 6LXB. *Stewart J. Brown*

ABOVE: Three Dominators entered service with London Buses in 1985 as part of what was described as the Alternative Vehicle Evaluation. They had Northern Counties bodies and were initially allocated to route 170, running between Aldwych and Roehampton. One is seen entering Trafalgar Square from Whitehall in the summer of 1986. David Cole

BELOW: In 1991 the three London Buses Dominators were transferred to the London Coaches fleet. Two had their centre exits removed and operated with London Coaches for two years, after which they were sold to Capital Citybus; the third – the one with a Maxwell gearbox – remained unused by London Coaches and was scrapped in 1992. Tony Wilson

**ABOVE:** Ipswich Borough Transport bought one Dennis Dominator in 1985, along with one Leyland Olympian – its first double-deckers since its final new Atlanteans in 1981. Both had 70-seat dual-door bodies by East Lancs. Note the narrow entrance.
Peter Rowlands

**RIGHT:** The last Dominators for South Yorkshire PTE were long-wheelbase models with coach-seated Alexander R-type bodies and Gardner 6LXCT engines. They were delivered in 1986. The longer R type body used the same size of windows as the standard version but with an additional short bay mid-wheelbase. Fastline was the name given to the PTE's limited-stop services.
Peter Rowlands

**ABOVE:** The final livery worn by Leicester CityBus's Dominators while the company was council-owned marked a reversion to the traditional maroon and cream, which was perhaps a little sombre after the previous red, cream and grey scheme. It was introduced in 1990. This is one of 13 East Lancs-bodied Dominators delivered in 1988, the first batch of a planned 65-bus order, seen in 1990 soon after receiving the new livery. Tony Wilson

**LEFT:** Kowloon Motor Bus was easily the biggest customer for the Dennis Dragon, which was a three-axle version of the Dominator. Most had Duple Metsec bodywork, as seen on this 1987 bus. Stewart J. Brown

**ABOVE:** The first Dominator for London Country South West was a long-wheelbase model with a coach-seated East Lancs body. It wore various liveries, including Green Line for a short spell, before being repainted in standard fleet colours in 1992 and fitted with bus seats.
Tony Wilson

**LEFT:** In 1988/9 Warrington Borough Transport took delivery of 11 long-wheelbase Dominators – nine buses and two coaches. All had East Lancs bodies. Two of the buses are seen approaching the town centre in 1995. Peter Rowlands

**ABOVE:** Warrington's two Dominator coaches, which arrived in 1988, were impressive-looking vehicles. They had 76 seats – 12 fewer than in the buses delivered at the same time – and were finished in the operator's CoachLines livery. Bodywork was by East Lancs.
Stewart J. Brown

**RIGHT:** The last Dominators for Southampton were eight delivered in 1988. Like previous deliveries they were bodied by East Lancs, although a rather ungainly appearance was created by fitting opening windows at the front of the upper deck, in lieu of the fixed double-curvature screens that were usually to be found on this style of body. The batch would be sold to Capital Citybus in 1992. Peter Rowlands

**LEFT:** Ipswich's second Dominator, received in 1988, had a rather more stylish East Lancs body than its first (illustrated on page 44), being fitted with curved windscreens and a conventional full-width entrance. It was sold to Thamesdown Transport in 2004, joining that operator's yellow-liveried Student Bus fleet. It was a 71-seater with Ipswich; a 76-seater with Thamesdown. Peter Rowlands

**BELOW:** Grimsby-Cleethorpes Transport was a late convert to the Dominator, taking its first – four Alexander-bodied 78-seaters – in 1989. Another three followed in 1990. Tony Wilson

**ABOVE:** North Western received 10 new East Lancs-bodied Dominators in 1989. One is pictured loading in St Helens. Stewart J. Brown

**LEFT:** In 1989 London Country South West took seven Dominators for London Transport tendered services. They had East Lancs bodies. Pictured at Hounslow bus station, this example displays the word 'BUS' alongside the LT roundel in the offside windscreen, lest any intending passenger should think it was some other type of vehicle. Stewart J. Brown

**RIGHT:** To mark 90 years of municipal transport in the city in 1989, Kingston-upon-Hull City Transport repainted this 1987 East Lancs-bodied Dominator in the stylish livery used until the late 1960s, which featured exuberant art-deco swoops. It proved wise to have marked 90 years, for the city's local transport would no longer be in council ownership by the time of its centenary. Peter Rowlands

**BELOW:** Thamesdown bought 29 new Dominators, the last being five East Lancs-bodied 76-seaters in 1990; here one of these loads in Fleming Way, adjacent to Swindon bus station, when new. Thamesdown named its buses after Swindon-built railway locomotives; this is Western Explorer, the name of a 1962 'Western'-class diesel-hydraulic. Stewart J. Brown

THIS PAGE: Six Dominators joined the Midland Red North fleet in 1990, four of them diverted from Crosville as a result of the transfer of part of that company's operations. All six had East Lancs bodywork, built to an overall height of 13ft 9in rather than the standard 14ft 6in. When new they were predominantly white (left), as seen here in Crewe, but in the mid-1990s the operator adopted a livery of overall red (below) which evoked memories of the original Midland Red company.
Cliff Beeton, Stewart J. Brown

**LEFT:** Bournemouth Transport bought its first Dominators in 1990, and by 1992 it was running 18. All had 80-seat East Lancs bodies. A 1990 bus is seen in the town centre in the summer of 1991.
Tony Wilson

**BELOW:** In 1991 GM Buses was evaluating different vehicle types, and purchased ten Dominators, ten Volvo Citybuses and five Scanias, all with Northern Counties bodies. The Dominators were 72-seaters with Gardner 6LXCT engines and were among the last to be bodied by Northern Counties.
Peter Rowlands

THIS PAGE; The only significant London order for Dominators was placed by Ensignbus, which took 24 in 1990/1. These were being delivered when the company was being taken over by the owners of Hong Kong Citybus, and most entered service in Ensign livery but with the addition of Citybus fleetnames, as seen here in Romford in the summer of 1991. They were soon repainted in yellow Capital Citybus colours. Bodywork was by Northern Counties.

Tony Wilson, Peter Rowlands

THIS PAGE: The early 1990s saw South Yorkshire extend its Mainline identity from Sheffield to embrace Rotherham and Doncaster. Here standard Alexander-bodied Dominators show (above) the grey-based scheme used in Doncaster and (left) the use of yellow with blue relief in Rotherham. Note that on both buses the paintshop has taken the trouble to pick out the lettering on the Dennis badge in a contrasting colour.
Tony Wilson (both)

**ABOVE:** In 1992 Stagecoach introduced the first new double-deck buses – Dennis Dragons – to Malawi. There were 10, with 108-seat Duple Metsec bodies and Inter-City Superdecker branding. Twenty similar buses would be delivered to Stagecoach Kenya in 1995/6. Stewart J. Brown collection

**BELOW:** A revised front panel and a BET-style double-curvature windscreen helped distinguish some of the later East Lancs copies of the Alexander R-type from the Scottish original. Four delivered to Grimsby-Cleethorpes in 1992 were that operator's last Dominators and brought the total in service to 15. Note the split-step entrance, a feature intended to make boarding and alighting easier for those with impaired mobility. Tony Wilson

**ABOVE:** Three Dominators which had been ordered by Strathclyde Buses were delivered to Mayne of Manchester. Fitted with East Lancs bodies, they entered service in 1993, but their stay in Manchester would be short, for at the end of 1995 they were sold to British Bus subsidiary Guildford & West Surrey. Tony Wilson

**BELOW:** After a two-year gap in production Dennis built its last four Dominators in 1996 for Guildford & West Surrey for use on a service between Guildford and Camberley on which there was an overhead obstruction. They had 76-seat East Lancs bodies and entered service in April 1996; this one is seen in Guildford when new. With the company having purchased Mayne's trio of 1993 Dominators, it had the last seven buses built. Stewart J. Brown

## Chapter Four

# FALCON EXTENDS THE RANGE

If the Dominator was a successor to the Fleetline, the Dennis Falcon was a successor to the Bristol RE. Ahead of the rear axle the Falcon was virtually identical to the Dominator – frame, steering, brakes were all the same. But behind the rear axle it had, for bus use as the Falcon H, a horizontal Gardner 6HLXB engine. The Falcon H had a Voith gearbox located ahead of the Dennis drop-centre rear axle, with a transfer box. Although leaf-spring suspension was listed as being available, all Falcons had air suspension.

ABOVE: The first Falcon was an H model for Leicester City Transport, fitted with a 51-seat Duple Dominant bus body. When new it was in Leicester's cream and maroon livery; this is a post-1983 view of it in the city council's corporate colours. A further six similar vehicles followed, but with 52 seats. All seven would be sold to Thamesdown Transport in 1987. Stewart J. Brown

The he first Falcon was completed in the spring of 1981 for Leicester City Transport, an enthusiastic Dominator user with almost 70 already in service (and more on order), and had an attractive 51-seat Duple Dominant bus body. Another six Duple-bodied Falcons were delivered to Leicester in 1983/4. All seven would be sold to Thamesdown Transport in 1987.

The second Falcon chassis was a Mercedes-Benz V6-engined model, hence the Falcon V designation. A 10.5m-long double-decker, it was fitted with the German company's OM421 11-litre engine and a Voith gearbox and featured a side-mounted radiator. Dennis's aim with the Falcon double-decker was a 10% improvement – cutting weight and cost by 10%, and increasing passenger capacity by the same figure. The first was fitted with an 84-seat East Lancs body and used as a Dennis demonstrator. Although completed at the end of 1981 it did not enter service until August 1982 and received a less than warm reception. When it was sold by Dennis less than 18 months later it was for use as a playbus by Stevenage Borough Council – an ignominious fate for such a young vehicle.

There was even a role for the Falcon V as a 12m-long high-floor coach – an unusual development

for what had started life as a rear-engined double-deck chassis. This was developed to meet the requirements of the National Bus Company, with an extended 6,096mm wheelbase, 260bhp V8 Perkins 10.5-litre TV8.640 engine and Voith D854 four-speed automatic gearbox with integral retarder. Ten were built, in 1982, and fitted with 47-seat Duple Goldliner bodies for operation on National Express Rapide services, the low chassis frame providing ample room for under-floor luggage lockers. They were operated by Western National (five), National Travel West (two), Yorkshire Traction (two) and West Yorkshire Road Car (one). However, the coach had not been properly developed and was a dramatic failure. There were problems with the Duple body, notably water leaks and inadequate heat insulation around the engine, while in the engine compartment a nylon pipe which formed part of the fuel line was prone to failure, spilling diesel on to the hot turbocharger, with predictably unfortunate results; two of the 10 Falcon V coaches were destroyed by fires in 1984.

Nottingham City Transport, always on the lookout for ways of maximising passenger capacity, saw an opportunity with the Falcon V and ordered two

**ABOVE: The second Falcon was this V model, which was built as a demonstrator and saw just 18 months' use as a bus in 1982/3 before being sold for conversion to a playbus. It had an 84-seat East Lancs body and is seen here in the summer of 1983 demonstrating to Chesterfield Transport, which did go on to buy nine Falcon H single-deckers.**
Stewart J. Brown

double-deckers, one of which was exhibited at the 1982 Commercial Motor Show. Placed in service at the start of 1983, they had 88-seat dual-door East Lancs bodies and were later modified by having the radiators relocated from the rear to the front. Nottingham did not buy any Dominators but would in 1996 take four examples of the new Dennis Arrow (like the Falcon, a single-decker modified for double-deck bodywork) before buying low-floor Tridents from 1999 to 2001.

Greater Manchester PTE, which was operating four Dominators, ordered three double-deck Falcon Vs for evaluation. The chassis numbers suggest they were built towards the end of 1982, but they were not bodied by Northern Counties until the spring of 1984, entering service at the PTE's Atherton depot after the original Falcon V double-deck demonstrator had actually been retired from service. The compact V6 engine allowed more space for seats on the lower saloon, and the GMPTE buses were 84-seaters. The Manchester Falcons allowed a direct comparison with standard types in the PTE fleet. Their 84 seats, albeit within a greater overall length, represented a significant increase over the 75 fitted to the PTE's Dominators (a 12% improvement), while despite their increased size the unladen weight of 9,900kg was broadly in line with other modern vehicles in the fleet: a 9.5m Olympian with 73 seats weighed 9,877kg. The three Falcons passed to GM Buses South when the PTE's bus operations were privatised in 1994.

In all just six Falcon V double-deckers were built – three each bodied by East Lancs and Northern Counties. One of its weaknesses was the engine, and a lack of support for it from Mercedes.

Sales of single-deck Falcons continued steadily rather than spectacularly. An alternative HC model was available from 1983 and had a simpler drivetrain with the Gardner engine and Voith gearbox driving directly to an Eaton rear axle, with no need for a

**ABOVE: The least successful of the Falcons were the 10 built as express coaches to meet a specification drawn up by the National Bus Company. They had Duple Goldliner bodies with 47 seats and a toilet. Two were operated by National Travel West on the Manchester–London Rapide service; this one is seen outside London's Victoria Coach Station in the spring of 1983, when the coach was just a few months old. The others were used on similar services linking the capital with Yorkshire and the West Country.** Tony Wilson

**LEFT: Nottingham City Transport took two Falcon Vs, which entered service in 1983. They had 88-seat dual-door bodies built by East Lancs to Nottingham's distinctive style. This is a 1989 view. Both buses would be sold in 1992 to Cedar Coaches of Bedford.** Tony Wilson

ABOVE: The biggest operator of Falcon V double-deckers – with just three – was Greater Manchester PTE. New in 1984, these were initially based at Atherton; this is a 1987 view in Leigh, at which time the PTE's bus operations were trading as GM Buses with local identities – in this case Atherleigh. These 10.5m-long buses were 84-seaters; the PTE's standard 9.5m Olympians seated 73.
Stewart J. Brown

transfer box. To accommodate this the rear overhang was extended from the 2,370mm of the H to 3,305mm. Ipswich Borough Transport was at the start of the 1980s running five ex-Leicester City Transport Bristol REs and expressed an interest in adding new ones to its fleet – something Leyland, with its focus on the National, was not willing to accommodate. So instead Ipswich evaluated a Leicester Falcon H and then ordered six HCs with East Lancs bodywork which were delivered in 1983. These had a steeply ramped floor which necessitated locating the exit immediately aft of the front wheel rather than in mid-wheelbase, and this became the standard Ipswich layout. There then followed some low-priced Leyland B21s, although to support its preferred long-term supplier Ipswich did in 1985 buy one Falcon. It then sustained Falcon production through the lean post-deregulation years, being the only buyer of Falcons in 1986 (seven), 1988 (four) and 1989 (seven). No Falcons were built in 1987. The

1986 buses had Northern Counties rather than East Lancs bodies and had Maxwell gearboxes.

Hartlepool Borough Transport, which in 1979 had bought six single-deck Dominators, then took one batch of Leyland National 2s in 1980 before returning to Dennis. It took six Falcon HCs in 1983 and another six in 1985, the first batch being bodied by Wadham Stringer, the second by Northern Counties. Grimsby Cleethorpes Transport also bought Wadham Stringer-bodied Falcons, taking four in 1983. Like the contemporary Leicester buses these were H models.

One Falcon HC was supplied to NBC. This was to have been bodied by Duple but was instead sent to Wadham Stringer. It had a 6HLX engine and was delivered to Alder Valley in 1983 in Londonlink livery. It was intended to evaluate the potential for a rear-engined Gardner-powered dual-purpose vehicle. It was also used to help the development of fire-retardant material – somewhat ironic, for the body was destroyed by fire in 1986. However, the chassis

was rebodied by Wadham Stringer, and the vehicle duly returned to service. It would later see further service with Mayne of Manchester.

Two other municipals bought Falcon HCs. Chesterfield had nine – four, with East Lancs bodies, delivered in 1983, followed by five Marshall-bodied buses in 1984; these were the only Marshall-bodied Falcons. Hyndburn, which was running Dominators, took two East Lancs-bodied Falcon HCs which were unusual in being short 10m models with 43 seats, in 1984/5. Chesterfield's four 1983 buses were later purchased by Ipswich for use on rural services.

Blackpool Transport, which had four Dennis Lancets, tried two Falcons in 1983 – one from Ipswich, the other from Chesterfield – but subsequently ordered Leyland National 2s with Gardner engines.

The best year for the Falcon in the UK was 1983, when 26 were delivered. Only eight entered service in Britain in 1984, although production was boosted by an order for 20 for Kowloon Motor Bus. These had

air-conditioned Duple Metsec coach bodies and were purchased for the Airbus airport service.

As mentioned above, only Ipswich was taking Falcons in the latter part of the 1980s, but in 1990 there came an order from Drawlane for 18 with 48-seat East Lancs bodies, the first examples of the builder's new EL2000 style. These went to London Country South West (10) and North Western (eight). Both companies were already running Dominators. Drawlane successor British Bus would take nine more at the start of 1993, for Midland Red North.

Leicester reappeared as the only Falcon buyer in 1991 and 1992, taking nine with East Lancs bodies. A further seven would follow, with Northern Counties bodywork, in 1993. These were to be the last Falcons. Total production was 139, comprising 10 National Express coaches, six double-deckers and 123 single-deckers, of which 20 were exported to Hong Kong.

The Falcon name, incidentally, revived that of a lightweight single-deck chassis, the last examples of which had been built in 1957.

**ABOVE: Ipswich was the biggest buyer of the Falcon, taking 25 in the period 1983-9. The first six had dual-door East Lancs bodies. The styling was odd, with the offset radiator and Dennis badge, and the combination of radiused corners on the main side windows and square corners for the small high-set windows in the first three bays. This one is seen in Hornchurch in 1992, operating on hire to Capital Citybus.**
Tony Wilson

**ABOVE:** Blackpool Transport tried two Falcons in 1983. This Ipswich bus is seen in Poulton-le-Fylde and shows clearly how the floor was ramped towards the rear, creating an effect which coach manufacturers would later describe as 'theatre-style seating'. After trying the Falcons Blackpool ordered Gardner-engined Leyland National 2s. Mark Bailey

**BELOW:** Hartlepool, which had six single-deck Dominators in operation, took six Falcons with Wadham Stringer Vanguard bodies in 1983. They were 46-seaters. Peter Rowlands

**ABOVE:** Wadham Stringer was also chosen by Grimsby-Cleethorpes to body its 1983 Falcons, which were of the rarer H design, with the gearbox ahead of the rear axle. Grimsby would later buy Dominator double-deckers and Lance single-deckers.
Tony Wilson

**LEFT:** Early Leyland National 2s with Leyland engines were not the most reliable of buses, and after taking a batch of National 2s in 1981, Chesterfield Transport switched to the Dennis Falcon. Its first four, in 1983, had high-floor East Lancs bodies.
David Cole

**RIGHT:** One Falcon HC was purchased by NBC and operated for Alder Valley, Dennis's local bus company. New in 1983, it had a dual-purpose Wadham Stringer body and was painted in Alder Valley's Londonlink livery, as seen here at Battersea coach park in 1984. Note the early form of electronic destination display. The body was destroyed by fire in 1986, and the chassis was rebodied by Wadham Stringer with a body identical to the original.
Tony Wilson

**LEFT:** Five Marshall-bodied Falcons were purchased by Chesterfield Corporation in 1984. They were 53-seaters. The body looked bland when compared with earlier Marshall single-deck bodies on Dominators, in part because of the plain grille. These were the only Falcons to be bodied by Marshall. Leyland's decision to offer Gardner engines in the National 2 would see Chesterfield switch back from Falcons to National 2s.
Peter Rowlands

**ABOVE:** Hyndburn Transport bought two East Lancs-bodied Falcons, one each in 1984 and 1985. Both were dual-purpose 43-seaters, with a high floor. The newer of the two is seen in Blackburn bus station in 1991. Mark Bailey

**BELOW:** Hartlepool's second and last batch of Falcons comprised six buses with angular Northern Counties bodywork, delivered in 1985. Mark Bailey

**RIGHT:** The Hartlepool operation was acquired by Stagecoach in 1995, when this newly repainted Falcon was photographed. Tony Wilson

**BELOW:** One East Lancs-bodied Falcon joined the Ipswich fleet in 1985, along with one Dominator. Ipswich buses were at this time named after Thames barges; this is Hobby. Tony Wilson

**LEFT:** In 1986 Ipswich took seven Falcons, and for the first time in its history ordered Northern Counties bodywork. Dual-door 45-seaters, they were broadly similar to buses delivered the previous year to Hartlepool.
Tony Wilson

**BELOW:** The final Ipswich Falcons, delivered in 1988/9, had dual-door East Lancs bodies. This 1989 bus was Ipswich's last Falcon.
Mark Bailey

**ABOVE:** In 1990 London Country South West took 10 Falcons, fitted with 48-seat East Lancs bodies. One is at West Croydon bus station soon after delivery, operating on a London Transport service to Purley. Similar buses were supplied to sister Drawlane company North Western at the same time, and to Midland Red North at the end of 1992. Tony Wilson

**LEFT:** Leicester CityBus was the last customer for the Falcon, taking 16 in the period 1991-3. Nine, including this 1991 bus, had East Lancs EL2000 bodies similar to those supplied to the Drawlane group. Mark Bailey

**ABOVE:** Northern Counties fitted its Paladin body to seven Falcons delivered to Leicester CityBus in 1993. Seen in 2004, this bus displays First's corporate fleetname and fleet number but retains Leicester's cream and red livery. Mark Bailey

**RIGHT:** Falcons were a popular second-hand buy, perhaps because of their Gardner engines. Mayne of Manchester operated this former Chesterfield bus, seen in Piccadilly Gardens in 1995. Tony Wilson

**ABOVE:** Islwyn Borough Transport acquired six of the former Leicester Falcons from Thamesdown in 1997. Most saw little use. This one is seen in Cardiff bus station soon after joining the Islwyn fleet. Mark Bailey

**LEFT:** The only Falcons exported new were a batch supplied to KMB in 1984. However, this Hyndburn bus saw further service overseas, on Malta – the Maltese Falcon – as seen here in the summer of 2010, by which time it was one of the very few Falcons still in operation. Mark Bailey

# Chapter Five
# THE DOMINO

The smallest of Dennis's heavy-duty 1980s bus chassis was the Domino, a midibus which was ahead of its time and over-engineered for the work required of it. The Domino had a rear-mounted Perkins 6.354 six-cylinder 5.8 litre engine and a Maxwell four-speed gearbox, and just 34 were built – 20 with stylish Northern Counties bodies for Greater Manchester PTE's Centreline inter station service in Manchester, and 14 with Optare bodies for South Yorkshire PTE. The South Yorkshire buses were shared between depots in Sheffield, Doncaster and Rotherham.

**ABOVE:** Greater Manchester PTE operated 20 Dominos with attractive Northern Counties steel-framed bodies. They were used on the Centreline service, which linked Manchester's two rail termini – Piccadilly and Victoria – for a flat fare of 30p.
Stewart J. Brown

A part-finished Greater Manchester Domino (it had no engine or gearbox) was exhibited at the 1984 Motor Show, although it would be the autumn of 1985 before any were delivered. The Domino was 7ft 6in wide and just over 25ft (7.6m) long. The Greater Manchester buses were 24-seaters with room for 14 standees; the South Yorkshire Dominos seated 33. One Greater Manchester bus was painted red and evaluated by London Buses' Abbey District alongside Bristol LHs on the C11 route between Archway and Brent Cross in North London for six months in 1985.

The South Yorkshire buses were withdrawn in 1991, eight briefly seeing further service with Stevensons of Uttoxeter. The Greater Manchester Dominos saw little use after 1990 and were stored until being sold in 1998 by Stagecoach Manchester (which had inherited them with the takeover of GM Buses South in 1996).

The Domino was too heavy (the Greater Manchester buses weighed 6,748kg) and too expensive but as a concept had much to commend it, as Dennis would later prove with the Dart, the most successful model in the company's history.

**ABOVE:** Before being delivered to Manchester one of the PTE's Dominos was evaluated by London Buses as a potential replacement for Bristol LHs on lightly used routes. It is seen here at Archway. London would indeed buy Dennis midibuses in large numbers – but not the over-engineered Domino.
Stewart J. Brown

**LEFT:** The Dominos for South Yorkshire were among the first buses to be bodied by Optare. They were to be found in Sheffield, Doncaster and, as seen here, Rotherham.
Stewart J. Brown

## Chapter Six

# THE ARROW TAKES OVER

Sales of Dominators had dropped sharply in the early 1990s. By the start of the decade the Gardner 6LXB engine which had held such appeal in the 1970s was looking outdated, and it was not going to be able to comply with new European exhaust-emissions limits. On top of that, building a specialised chassis in small numbers is not the most efficient method of manufacturing. So Dennis came up with a novel solution – to adapt its single-deck Lance chassis for double-deck use.

**ABOVE: How the Lance was originally conceived – as a single-deck bus. Northern Counties bodywork was fitted to this vehicle, one of 13 delivered to Eastern National in 1997. These were the last Lances for a British operator.** Stewart J. Brown

The Lance had been unveiled by Dennis at Coach & Bus '91 and was available with two wheelbases, for single-deck bodywork of 10.5m or 11.5m length, giving buyers of the successful Dart midibus the opportunity to buy larger single-deckers from the same stable. It was powered by a 211bhp 8.3-litre Cummins C series Euro 2 engine and had a ZF 4HP500 automatic gearbox. The Lance met Euro 2 emissions limits 12 months before they came in to effect. The compact engine was mounted in line with the chassis, eliminating the need for the angle drive that was a feature of the Dominator and other transverse-rear-engined double-deckers. The radiator was also mounted at the rear.

At Coach & Bus '95 Dennis announced the availability of the Lance as a double-decker, using the shorter of the two available wheelbases, 5,050mm, with uprated suspension incorporating an anti-roll bar and a marginal increase in engine power, to 215bhp. The rear overhang was reduced from 2,823mm on the single-decker to 2,310mm. The first bus, for Nottingham City Transport, was a show exhibit and had a 79-seat Northern Counties Palatine II body, in which all of the seats were forward-facing – one benefit of having a relatively high chassis frame. It weighed 10,840kg and was just under 10.5m long. The chassis weighed 5,610kg, which was considerably less than a comparable long-wheelbase Dominator at 6,760kg, thanks in part to the lighter engine and the absence of an angle drive.

At the launch Dennis stated that the Lance would prove to be the most cost-effective double-decker on the market, arguing that the straightforward driveline would cut maintenance costs, while the low weight and high carrying capacity would maximise earning potential. That was all well and good, but a clue that the Lance might not be the future of double-deck design was also at Coach & Bus '95 in the shape of the first of a new generation of low-floor double-deck chassis being exhibited by DAF.

Dennis very quickly had a rethink on the name and in the spring of 1996 decided that the double-deck Lance would be known as the Arrow, maintaining a policy of naming its vehicles after sharp projectiles. The second builder to body the chassis was East Lancs, and on a bus for London & Country (as London Country South West had by now been formally retitled) it got the unladen weight down to just over 10 tonnes, allowing the bus to carry 100 people – 84 seated and 16 standing.

Arrows entered service with four operators in 1996. Capital Citybus took 16 (with delivery running into the early months of 1997), London & Country had 10 (delivered along with the last four Dominators for Guildford & West Surrey), Nottingham City Transport had four (including the show vehicle), and Aintree Coachline bought one, primarily for a school

contract. The London & Country buses were ordered to provide commonality with 15 Lance single-deckers delivered at the same time and had East Lancs bodies. All the other 1996 Arrows were bodied by Northern Counties to its Palatine II design, and all but the first two for Nottingham were part of a batch of 20 built as stock vehicles.

In 1997 the only operator to take Arrows was Capital Citybus, and these featured a new style of East Lancs body, the Pyoneer. This was developed from the 1995 Cityzen body which had been available

**ABOVE:** The Arrow – initially still called Lance – was launched at Coach & Bus 95 with this bus (top) for Nottingham City Transport. It was one of four with Northern Counties Palatine II bodywork, all of which entered service in the spring of 1996. The later buses (bottom) were in fleet livery. All four would be sold to Aintree Coachline in 2005.
Tony Wilson (both)

solely on Scania N113 chassis. Capital Citybus became the biggest user of the Arrow, building up a fleet of 54 by the summer of 1998 when the last four, with S registrations, entered service. The company claimed that fuel consumption for the Arrows was 2mpg better than on other types in its fleet.

Aintree Coachline took a second Arrow, this time with East Lancs body, in 1998, and one was delivered to London Traveller of Park Royal for private-hire and contract operation, this having an East Lancs body with 76 coach seats fitted with seat belts. Two Arrows were bought by playbus groups, one each bodied by East Lancs and Northern Counties, the latter being the last of the 20 stock buses which were thus shared between Capital Citybus (16), Nottingham (two), Aintree Coachline (one) and Waveney Playbus.

Despite having an anti-roll bar fitted to the chassis the Arrow was inclined to sway, and in response to

complaints from operators Dennis stiffened the suspension. This cured the problem but created another, causing the failure of chassis outriggers. Eventually the issue was resolved, and the Arrows settled down to give trouble-free service.

Total Arrow output was 73. The first entered service in April 1996, the last in August 1998. The last UK Lances, from which the Arrow had been developed, were delivered almost 18 months earlier than the last Arrows, in the spring of 1997. (A final batch of 20 Lance chassis was supplied to Singapore in 2000.)

The model which succeeded the Arrow was the low-floor Trident, and the first of these – destined to be the most successful double-decker in Dennis's history – entered service in 1999. In 18 years Dennis sold just under 1,000 Dominators to British bus operators. It would sell 1,000 Tridents in little more than 18 months.

ABOVE: The last two of the 10 Arrows delivered to London & Country were 76-seat coaches and wore a different livery, which would have Countryliner branding added to the upper-deck side panels. These vehicles were fitted with five-speed ZF gearboxes, whereas the buses that accompanied them had four-speed gearboxes. Stewart J. Brown

LEFT: Aintree Coachline's first Arrow was delivered with Lance badges, as seen here when the bus was new. It had an 84-seat Northern Counties Palatine II body and came from a batch of 20 vehicles built for the manufacturer's stock. Stewart J. Brown

**ABOVE:** The biggest Arrow operator was Capital Citybus, which took 54 of the 73 built. The first batch of 16 had single-door Northern Counties bodies from the 20 buses built for stock and included five which were delivered in an orange-based livery for operation on services replacing the East London Underground line which was closed for modernisation. Here (top) a brand-new bus waits at Surrey Quays on the ELX service from Aldgate in October 1996. The remaining 11 were in fleet livery; this view (bottom) dates from 2000 – note the corporate First name on the front. Tony Wilson

THIS PAGE: Subsequent Arrow deliveries to Capital Citybus had dual-door East Lancs bodies. The 1997 deliveries were in the company's established yellow livery and were operated on suburban services. Those which followed in 1998 were used on services running in to the centre of London and featured a revised colour scheme to meet London Transport's requirement that buses running into the central area be 80% red. The stylised 'C' logos on either side of the destination display were illuminated at night.
Stewart J. Brown, Peter Rowlands

ABOVE: Two Arrows were built as bespoke playbuses, one by Northern Counties and the other, seen here at Duxford in 1999, by East Lancs. The Pyramids Playbus organisation was based in Thorndon, near Eye, in Suffolk. Tony Wilson

BELOW: In 1998 London Traveller purchased a solitary Arrow which had a coach-seated East Lancs body. It was used for private hires and on rail-replacement services. Tony Wilson

ABOVE: Aintree Coachline's second Arrow, with East Lancs Pyoneer body, pauses outside Pleasureland in Southport. It was new in 1998. Tony Wilson

LEFT: First acquired the 54 Arrows operated by Capital Citybus, and these were later transferred to the group's provincial fleets, all ending up with First Manchester, which was still operating a few of them in 2012. An East Lancs-bodied bus, converted to single-door, is seen in Leigh in 2008. Mark Bailey

# Chapter Seven
# IN LATER LIFE

Each of the three of the big groups which evolved in the 1990s – Arriva, First and Stagecoach – operated Dennis models from the Dominator period. Arriva inherited Dominators from former Drawlane companies, and the newest of these lasted well into the 21st century, late survivors running for its Southern Counties fleets. Most of the North Western Dominators were transferred to Arriva Southend in 1999, surviving there until 2006/7, while the group's last surviving Dominators, three of the four which had been new to Guildford & West Surrey in 1996, were still in service with Arriva Kent & Sussex in Maidstone in 2012. Its Falcons too were long-lived, the last running for Arriva Midlands North. The 10 Arrows delivered to Guildford & West Surrey were also inherited by Arriva, initially remaining in the South but in 1999 moving to Arriva Yorkshire.

**ABOVE:** In 1998 Stagecoach shipped 20 Dennis Dragons from Nairobi to Manchester for use on Magic Bus services in the city. The Dragons were just two years old and had Duple Metsec bodies. For service in Manchester they were fitted with new seats and heaters. The last were withdrawn in 2010.
Stewart J. Brown

First acquired most of the Arrows which had been built when it purchased Capital Citybus. The same company also provided the group with Dominators, as did the two biggest Dominator buyers, South Yorkshire and Leicester, both of which became First subsidiaries. Some ex-Leicester Dominators saw service with First Northampton. First also acquired Falcons with the Leicester business. The last of the South Yorkshire Dominators were withdrawn in the summer of 2006. Most of the former Capital Citybus Dominators – 21 of the 24 – were transferred to First Glasgow in 2002. A few of the ex-Capital Citybus Arrows survived in service with First Manchester in 2012.

Capital Citybus had in 1992 acquired all eight Dominators delivered to Southampton in 1988, and put them to use on a London Transport contracted service. They moved north in 2000, being transferred to First Mainline (as the former South Yorkshire PTE operation was now known) and First PMT. Other second-hand acquisitions by Capital Citybus included Dominators from London Coaches (two, in 1993), Mainline in Sheffield (three, in 1994), Kelvin Central (nine, in 1995) and Leicester CityBus (seven, in 1996). The Kelvin Central buses were from the batch of 10 delivered to Merseyside PTE in 1982 and had been running in Scotland since 1992. In all, 29 Dominators were acquired from other operators by Capital Citybus.

Dominators inherited by Stagecoach were those operated by GM Buses South, Cleveland Transit, Kingston-upon-Hull and Grimsby-Cleethorpes. Falcons were still running at Hartlepool and Grimsby-Cleethorpes when Stagecoach took over, duly receiving Stagecoach corporate livery. The group also repatriated Dragons from Africa, using buses from Kenya on Magic Bus services in Manchester.

**BELOW: All 51 of Hull's Dominators passed to Stagecoach when it acquired the business in 1994. Three of the 15 vehicles delivered in the winter of 1985/6 had coach-style East Lancs bodies with 71 seats, and one is seen here in 1997, freshly repainted in Stagecoach corporate livery.** Tony Wilson

ABOVE: **The 30 Dominators purchased by Greater Manchester in 1985 were inherited by GM Buses South when the PTE fleet was split in 1993 and thus became part of Stagecoach when it acquired the company in 1996. One sparkles in the Manchester sun in the summer of 1999.** Stewart J. Brown

Thamesdown acquired many second-hand Dennises. In the 1980s it bought Dominators from East Staffordshire and Derby, and all seven of Leicester's Falcons; then, in 1998/9, it purchased six of the Dominators that had been new in 1989 to London Country South West. Chester also bought second-hand Dominators, and its fleet included buses that had been new to A1, Blackburn, Darlington, Hyndburn, Leicester and Merthyr Tydfil. Warrington bought Dominators from Blackburn and Leicester.

In the 1990s Dominators were a common sight on London Pride sightseeing work, most of them converted to part open-top layout. London Pride

acquired Dominators from Hull, Thamesdown, Eastbourne, Cleveland Transit and Kelvin Central, those from the last-named being former Central SMT buses.

Within the Scottish Bus Group there was in the late 1980s some redistribution of Central's Dominators, which saw examples running for Eastern (four), Lowland (three), and Kelvin (22). Kelvin and Central were merged as Kelvin Central in 1989, with a total of 44 Dominators; all were withdrawn by 1995. The four Eastern buses were only operated for a few months in 1986 before moving to Clydeside. Most of Clydeside's Dominators were sold to Hong Kong in 1993.

**ABOVE:** Arriva predecessor British Bus had 27 Falcons with East Lancs EL2000 bodies, and these received Arriva's corporate livery. They included nine that had been new to Midland Red North in the winter of 1992/3, one of which is seen with Arriva Midlands North in Bridgnorth in 2002. Mark Bailey

**BELOW:** The 10 Arrows operated by London & Country headed north in 1999 under Arriva ownership, joining the group's Yorkshire business. This one was photographed in Leeds in 2003. Mark Bailey

**LEFT:** Capital Citybus built up a large fleet of second-hand Dominators for operation on London contracts. This East Lancs-bodied bus came from Leicester CityBus. The last Capital Citybus Dominators departed London in 2002, by which time the company was part of FirstGroup. Stewart J. Brown

**BELOW:** When it secured a new London Transport contract in 1992 Capital Citybus purchased eight Dominators from Southampton CityBus. They had East Lancs bodywork. One is seen at Whipps Cross soon after joining the Capital Citybus fleet. Tony Wilson

ABOVE: Two of the three Dominators purchased by London Buses as part of its Alternative Vehicle Evaluation programme were later operated by Capital Citybus. This one was photographed in Romford in 1995. David Cole

RIGHT: Most of Capital Citybus's Dominators were transferred to other FirstGroup operators. This one-time Southampton bus is seen fresh from the PMT paintshop with Crosville fleetnames at the company's Adderley Green depot in 2000. Cliff Beeton

**THIS PAGE:** Chester City Transport acquired Dominators from a wide range of operators. This East Lancs-bodied bus (above) was new to Blackburn in 1981, while the Marshall-bodied single-decker (left) was one of three which came from Merthyr Tydfil in 1985.
Cliff Beeton, Peter Rowlands

**ABOVE:** Leicester CityBus was purchased by GRT, one of the constituents of FirstGroup, in 1993. GRT adopted a subtle approach to a corporate identity, employing a standard livery layout throughout its fleets, but with colours which recognised the heritage of each individual business. The Leicester CityBus version featured two shades of red, as seen on a 1982 East Lancs-bodied Dominator in 1995. Tony Wilson

**BELOW:** Kelvin Central Buses was formed in 1989 by the merger of the Central Scottish and Kelvin Scottish businesses and inherited 44 of the 51 Dominators that had been purchased by Central between 1978 and 1983. KCB initially adopted an unusual application of red and cream for its livery, as seen here on a 1982 Dominator heading towards central Glasgow. Stewart J. Brown

**ABOVE:** Most of South Yorkshire's Dominators were still in service when First acquired the business in 1998. This 1985 Alexander-bodied bus was photographed running in corporate colours for First Mainline in Doncaster in 2001. The last of the South Yorkshire Dominators would survive until 2006. Mark Bailey

**BELOW:** Second-hand Dominators were regular performers on the London Pride sightseeing tour in the 1990s. Pictured crossing London Bridge in the summer of 1996, this former Cleveland Transit bus has been converted to partial open-top and fitted with an offside door. Tony Wilson

RIGHT: To mark the centenary of municipal transport in Doncaster in 2002, First South Yorkshire repainted a Dominator in the final version of Doncaster Corporation's livery – but chose an odd bus in the fleet. The Doncaster centenary Dominator was one of five in the First South Yorkshire fleet which had been new to Southampton CityBus in 1988 and reached Yorkshire via Capital Citybus. It had an East Lancs body. In this view a T-shaped advertisement unfortunately conceals the purple relief band which sweeps down behind the driver's side window and was a feature of the final Doncaster livery. Tony Wilson

LEFT: The last Dominators in regular service with a major group were still running for Arriva Kent & Sussex in 2012. These were three of the last four Dominators built and had been new to Guildford & West Surrey in 1996. This one is seen in Tunbridge Wells in December 2011. Richard Lewis

## Chapter Eight

# THE DOMINATOR – A TURNING-POINT FOR DENNIS

The Dominator was one of the most important models in Dennis's history. The company's involvement in the bus and coach market had not been marked with conspicuous success in the years from the end of World War 2. Its truck sales were steady rather than spectacular. And while the Dennis name was synonymous with fire appliances, that was a small and specialised business.

**ABOVE: The Dominator laid the foundation for Dennis's growth in the bus business. Its most successful model was the Dart, which was bought by operators large and small. This Duple-bodied demonstrator was the first to enter service, with London Central, at the end of 1989 and is seen in Peckham in its first week in service.** Stewart J. Brown

The Dominator established Dennis as a credible builder of urban buses. And, more importantly, it led to other models which built on the Dominator's success. Most obviously there were the three-axle variants for Hong Kong, which became a major market for the company, and remains so for its successor, Alexander Dennis. It also gave Dennis the impetus to try to replicate the model's success in other market segments. For coach operators Dennis developed the Dorchester and the lighter Lancet, both of which sold in small numbers. But it then moved on to the Javelin, which enjoyed high sales in its early years, as well as a production run which started in 1987 and continued until 2011.

The Javelin used a Cummins engine, and from that point Cummins became the company's preferred engine supplier. The next new models, the Dart and Lance single-deckers, were designed around Cummins engines. The Dart became one of the most successful bus designs of recent times. For a period in the late 1980s most new buses for London were Darts, and the low-entry version, the Dart SLF (Super Low Floor) was the first cost-effective accessible bus in Britain.

Against this background the Dominator continued in production, although it was a design from an earlier era. The Arrow which followed it can be seen with hindsight as an interim model. The real successor to the Dominator was the low-floor Trident, which repeated the sales success of the Dart. The impact of the Trident was enormous.

Where the Dominator secured some of its business from disaffected Leyland customers, the Trident appeared at a time when Volvo, successor to Leyland as the main supplier of double-deck buses in Britain, seriously misjudged the market.

Dennis had, with the Dart, demonstrated its ability to build reliable buses and to provide their operators with proper technical and after-sales support. This was a solid platform from which to launch the Trident. And with the Trident Dennis had designed a bus specifically for the needs of British operators. Volvo, by contrast, had hoped to sell a modified European citybus chassis, the B7L, and when this was rejected by operators Volvo lost valuable time designing a more appropriate bus, which would appear as the B7TL. That mistake cost Volvo its leadership in double-deck sales, as operators which had been buying Volvo Olympians switched to Dennis Tridents. A three-axle version of the Trident maintained Dennis's position in Hong Kong.

There followed a troubled period in the early years of the 21st century. Dennis and coachbuilder Alexander were united as TransBus. That collapsed, but from the ruins there arose a new company, Alexander Dennis, which today builds the highly successful Enviro range of urban buses, the chassis for which are still produced in Guildford.

Had the Dominator not paved the way, it is difficult to imagine how any of this would have happened.

**BELOW:** With the low-floor Trident Dennis successfully challenged Volvo's supremacy in the supply of double-deckers. At Stagecoach London in January 1999 the change is illustrated by a brand-new Trident with 73-seat Alexander ALX400 body alongside a 1998 Volvo Olympian with Alexander R-type body seating 79. With the Trident Dennis supplanted Volvo as Stagecoach's principal supplier of double-deckers. Stewart J. Brown

**ABOVE:** Today's Alexander Dennis Enviro400 maintains Dennis's presence in the British bus market and, like the Trident before it, has a Cummins engine. A First Glasgow Enviro400 is seen soon after delivery in 2011. The silver livery was used for buses – some of which were hybrid Enviro400H models – on a busy cross-city service. Stewart J. Brown

# APPENDICES

## UK Dennis Dominator deliveries 1977-96

| | 1977 | 1978 | 1979 | 1980 | 1981 | 1982 | 1983 | 1984 | 1985 | 1986 | 1987 | 1988 | 1989 | 1990 | 1991 | 1992 | 1993 | 1994 | 1995 | 1996 | Total |
|---|---|---|---|---|---|---|---|---|---|---|---|---|---|---|---|---|---|---|---|---|---|
| South Yorkshire PTE | 1 | 1 | | 2 | 55 | 119 | 40 | 64 | 18† | 23 | | | | | | | | | | | 323 |
| Leicester City Transport | 1 | 24 | 11 | 23 | 18 | 20 | 9 | 4 | 4 | 4* | | 13 | 13 | | | | | | | | 144 |
| PMT | | 1 | | | | | | | | | | | | | | | | | | | 1 |
| East Staffordshire District Council | | 2 | 3 | 5 | 5 | | | | | | | | | | | | | | | | 15 |
| Central SMT | | 1 | | | 20 | 20 | 10 | | | | | | | | | | | | | | 51 |
| Cardiff City Transport | | 1 | | | | | | | | | | | | | | | | | | | 1 |
| Darlington Borough Transport | | | 10* | 8* | | | | | | | | | | | | | | | | | 18 |
| Blackburn Borough Transport | | | 2 | 5 | | | | | | | | | | | | | | | | | 7 |
| Hyndburn Borough Transport | | | 1 | 2 | 2 | | 1 | 1 | 2 | | | | | | | | | | | | 9 |
| Tayside Regional Council | | | 1 | 5 | | | | | | | | | | | | | | | | | 6 |
| Hartlepool Borough Transport | | | 6* | | | | | | | | | | | | | | | | | | 6 |
| Barrow Borough Transport | | | 2* | | | | | | | | | | | | | | | | | | 2 |
| A1, Ardrossan | | | 2 | 1 | 1 | | | | | | | | | | | | | | | | 4 |
| Merthyr Tydfil Borough Transport | | | 6* | | | | | | | | | | | | | | | | | | 6 |
| Greater Manchester PTE | | | | 2 | 2 | | | | 30 | | | | | | | | | | | | 34 |
| OK, Bishop Auckland | | | | 1 | | | | | | | | | | | | | | | | | 1 |
| Maidstone & District | | | | 6 | | | | | | | | | | | | | | | | | 6 |
| Tyne & Wear Fire Service | | | | 1ø | | | | | | | | | | | | | | | | | 1 |
| Derby City Transport | | | | 3 | 3 | | | | | | | | | | | | | | | | 6 |
| Cleveland Transit | | | | 2 | | | 9 | 3 | 5 | 4 | | | | | | | | | | | 23 |
| Merseyside PTE | | | | 5 | | 10 | | | | | | | | | | | | | | | 15 |
| AA, Ayr | | | | 1 | | 1 | | | | | | | | | | | | | | | 2 |
| Thamesdown Transport | | | | 4* | 5 | 5 | 4 | 5 | 5 | | | | | | | | | | | | 28 |
| Chester City Transport | | | | | 5 | 6 | 3 | | | | | | | | | | | | | | 14 |
| Eastbourne Borough Council | | | | | 4 | 5 | | | | | | | | | | | | | | | 9 |
| Brighton Borough Transport | | | | | 2 | | | | 4 | | | | | | | | | | | | 6 |
| Warrington Borough Transport | | | | | | 4 | 4 | | | | | 6 | 5 | | | | | | | | 19 |
| Western SMT | | | | | | | 12 | | | | | | | | | | | | | | 12 |
| Southampton City Transport | | | | | | | | 1 | | 4 | | 8 | | | | | | | | | 13 |
| London Transport | | | | | | | | 3 | | | | | | | | | | | | | 3 |
| Kingston-upon-Hull City Transport | | | | | | | | 10 | 2 | 13 | 10 | 10 | 6 | | | | | | | | 51 |
| Ipswich Borough Transport | | | | | | | | | 1 | | | 1 | | | | | | | | | 2 |
| Clydeside Scottish | | | | | | | | | 12 | | | | | | | | | | | | 12 |
| London Country South West | | | | | | | | | | | | 1 | 8 | | | | | | | | 9 |
| Grimsby-Cleethorpes Transport | | | | | | | | | | | | | 4 | 3 | 4 | 4 | | | | | 15 |
| North Western | | | | | | | | | | | | | 10 | 8 | | | | | | | 18 |
| Midland Red North | | | | | | | | | | | | | | 6 | | | | | | | 6 |
| Bournemouth Transport | | | | | | | | | | | | | | 7 | 7 | 4 | | | | | 18 |
| Ensignbus | | | | | | | | | | | | | | 1 | 23 | | | | | | 24 |
| GM Buses | | | | | | | | | | | | | | | 10 | | | | | | 10 |
| Capital Citybus | | | | | | | | | | | | | | | 2 | | | | | | 2 |
| Mayne, Manchester | | | | | | | | | | | | | | | | | 3 | | | | 3 |
| Guildford & West Surrey | | | | | | | | | | | | | | | | | | | | 4 | 4 |
| **Total** | **2** | **30** | **44** | **64** | **127** | **192** | **92** | **91** | **83** | **48** | **10** | **39** | **46** | **30** | **46** | **8** | **3** | **-** | **-** | **4** | **959** |

* single-deck
ø non-PSV
† includes one trolleybus which never operated in service

# UK Dennis Falcon deliveries 1981-93

| | 1981 | 1982 | 1983 | 1984 | 1985 | 1986 | 1987 | 1988 | 1989 | 1990 | 1991 | 1992 | 1993 | Total |
|---|---|---|---|---|---|---|---|---|---|---|---|---|---|---|
| Leicester City Transport | 1 | | 3 | 3 | | | | | | | 6 | 3 | 7 | 23 |
| Dennis (demonstrator) | | 1* | | | | | | | | | | | | 1 |
| Western National | | 5† | | | | | | | | | | | | 5 |
| Yorkshire Traction | | 2† | | | | | | | | | | | | 2 |
| West Yorkshire RCC | | 1† | | | | | | | | | | | | 1 |
| National Travel West | | 2† | | | | | | | | | | | | 2 |
| Nottingham City Transport | | | 2* | | | | | | | | | | | 2 |
| Greater Manchester PTE | | | | 3* | | | | | | | | | | 3 |
| Ipswich Borough Transport | | | 6 | | 1 | 7 | | 4 | 7 | | | | | 25 |
| Hartlepool Borough Transport | | | 6 | | 6 | | | | | | | | | 12 |
| Grimsby-Cleethorpes | | | 4 | | | | | | | | | | | 4 |
| Chesterfield Transport | | | 4 | 5 | | | | | | | | | | 9 |
| Alder Valley | | | 1 | | | | | | | | | | | 1 |
| Hyndburn Borough Transport | | | | 1 | 1 | | | | | | | | | 2 |
| London Country South West | | | | | | | | | | 10 | | | | 10 |
| North Western | | | | | | | | | | 8 | | | | 8 |
| Midland Red North | | | | | | | | | | | | 9 | | 9 |
| **Total** | **1** | **11** | **26** | **12** | **8** | **7** | **-** | **4** | **7** | **18** | **6** | **12** | **7** | **119** |

* double-deck
† coach

# Dennis Arrow deliveries 1996-8

| | 1996 | 1997 | 1998 | Total |
|---|---|---|---|---|
| London & Country | 10 | | | 10 |
| Nottingham City Transport | 4 | | | 4 |
| Capital Citybus | 12 | 14 | 28 | 54 |
| Aintree Coachline, Bootle | 1 | | 1 | 2 |
| London Traveller, Harlesden | | | 1 | 1 |
| Pyramids Playbus, Thorndon | | 1 | | 1 |
| Waveney Playbus | | 1 | | 1 |
| **Total** | **27** | **16** | **30** | **73** |